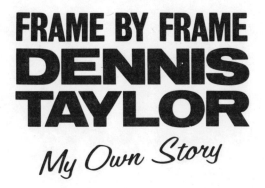

FRAME BY FRAME
DENNIS TAYLOR

My Own Story

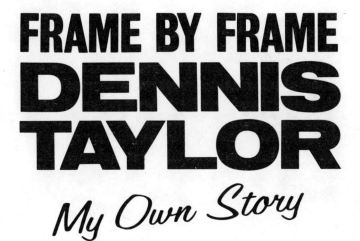

FRAME BY FRAME
DENNIS TAYLOR

My Own Story

Macdonald
Queen Anne Press

For Trish and my mother,
the two most important women
in my life.

A *Queen Anne Press* BOOK

© Dennis Taylor 1985

First published in 1985 by Queen Anne Press,
a division of Macdonald & Co (Publishers) Ltd,
Maxwell House, 74 Worship Street, London EC2A 2EN
A BPCC plc Company

British Library Cataloguing in Publication Data

Taylor, Dennis
    Frame by frame : the autobiography of Dennis
    Taylor.
    1. Taylor, Dennis   2. Snooker players—Great
    Britain—Biography
    I. Title
    794.7'35'0924   GV900.S6

    ISBN 0-356-12179-8

Photoset in North Wales by
Derek Doyle & Associates, Mold, Clwyd
Printed and bound in Great Britain by
Biddles Ltd, Guildford

CONTENTS

ACKNOWLEDGEMENTS

I should like to thank all my family and friends, especially my father and my four sisters, for helping me to recall the early days. Acknowledgements are also due to Clive Everton of *Snooker Scene* and to the other journalists who are quoted in the book, notably John 'Cueman' Taylor of the *Lancashire Evening Telegraph*. I am grateful also to Trevor East and Barry Hearn for their encouragement, and to Donald Trelford of the *Observer* for helping me to frame my thoughts, so to speak, frame by frame. If any of my colleagues on the circuit feel that I have miscued in their direction, they will doubtless have every chance to snooker me back!

PART ONE

An Irish Boy (1949-66)

At 22 minutes past midnight on Monday, 29 April 1985 I potted the black to win a game of snooker. I'd done it thousands of times before. But never like this.

As the audience in Sheffield's Crucible Theatre rose to their feet to salute the most exciting game of snooker they had ever seen, I raised the cue above my head tightly in both hands like a weight-lifter. What I had snatched was nothing less than the championship of the world – a title that mattered even more than the purse that went with it of £60,000.

It had taken me a long time to get there, which made it all the sweeter. It had taken me thirteen years to become an overnight success. That was how long I had been a professional player. To be more exact, though, it was twenty-seven years since I had peeped through a door at Gervin's club at Coalisland, County Tyrone, in the North of Ireland, and gazed in boyish wonder at the coloured balls whizzing around. I never dreamt then, though, that the game I was watching would one night take me to the top of the world.

And the whole world seems to have been looking on that night. Nearly twenty million people in Britain alone – 45 per cent of all households, the biggest TV audience ever for a sporting event – had stayed out of bed as I agonisingly inched my way back on level terms with Steve Davis, the reigning world champion, and then went ahead – for the first and only time in the match – with the very last shot of the very last frame of all.

As that crucial black stayed out of the pocket for six desperate attempts until I sank it with the seventh, I couldn't help thinking back to those early days at Gervin's, when we used to *avoid* potting the black to keep the game going, because we couldn't afford a shilling for another one. I remember the owner, Jim-Joe Gervin, leaning over and warning us with the feather duster he always carried in his hand: 'One day you'll need the black and you'll regret all this messing about.'

They say that a drowning man's past life all comes up before him. I wasn't exactly drowning in the Crucible, but there were times when it must have seemed like that – especially when I went 0-8 down and took over six hours to win my first frame! My past life certainly swam before me then – and, of course, my present life, with my wife, my children, my sisters and their husbands, all sitting in the arena with their fingers crossed (and, I expect, everything else), hardly daring to watch. One of the Coalisland contingent actually fell off the seat with a crash when I won and my sister Brenda's husband was nearly sent out by referee John Williams for whistling in sheer excitement.

My father, Tommy, was back home in Mourne Crescent, Coalisland, just up the hill from Gervin's, holding his breath as he watched it all on TV. My greatest sadness that night was that my mother, Annie, my keenest fan, couldn't be there. She had suddenly died a few months before. A week before her death she had said: 'I wish our Dennis would get a title. He'll get it one day, but I may not be here to see it.' And even so my sister Margaret swears Annie was there in the Crucible

8

with her that night, spiriting that black ball into the hole.

It was over an hour later – at 1.40 a.m. precisely – when I got a telephone call through to my father. 'Listen to this,' he said, and held the receiver so that I could hear the noise in the Coalisland streets. It was incredible. Car horns were blaring into the night as whole families came out – some in pyjamas and dressing-gowns – and paraded around the town square and then up to Mourne Crescent, the family home. Nobody slept that night in Coalisland – and it was bad luck on anybody who tried! The whole town was just too excited to go to bed.

The scenes in Gervin's club were equally amazing. A local TV engineer, Peter McIlroy, had the foresight to make an amateur video film of that night which had me laughing and crying when I saw it later. People poured out into the streets singing and dancing in spontaneous joy.

The air was filled with the strains of 'Here we go, here we go, here we go', and some lads from the local brass band brought out their instruments, including a French horn, for a boozy blow in the night air. People wandered about the streets for hours on end clutching glasses and each other. Boys climbed on their fathers' shoulders to see the remarkable sight. Whole families hugged each other. A big bald man lay drunk in the road and nobody took any notice, the traffic moved round him like a traffic island. The priest was out there, too, joining in the general celebrations.

It was open house in Mourne Crescent, with my father rushed off his feet by visitors. The door-bell and the phone never stopped ringing till dawn. Even on Monday morning the sun came up to reveal people still walking around in a daze as if they didn't want the party ever to come to an end.

A friend of mine, Pat Logan, whose family own the local paper, *The Democrat*, said: 'This is a fairy tale come true. It's the nicest thing that ever happened to the people of Coalisland. They've had little enough in their lives to cheer about.' I have to admit that I was nearly choked with pride when I heard that – and my glasses needed windscreen wipers.

A week later I was due to make a hero's return to Coalisland, where a civic reception had been arranged. I had gone forward to sit with the pilot as we flew over to Belfast and could see the storm clouds gathering. 'This is going to be terrible for everyone if it rains,' I said to my wife Patricia (who is better known to everybody as Trish). It was pouring down on our car all the way from Belfast to Dungannon. I needn't have worried, though, because the sun suddenly shone through, almost miraculously, just as we reached Coalisland itself. It was quite incredible. People in the town were to attribute this to my late mother's influence in high places – 'Annie Taylor will have put a word in His ear,' they said.

That wasn't the only miracle. The *Irish Independent* reported on its front page the next day: 'As Taylor, holding the trophy aloft, drew into sight of the town square for the first time, his jaw dropped at just how many people awaited him. Then he picked out this one and that one he knew, waving or calling out a greeting.' The paper said there were over ten thousand people, Catholic and Protestant, crowded into that square – it's no wonder my jaw dropped!

It was even more of a shock for Trish and the children – Denise, Damian and Brendan – because they have lived all their lives in Blackburn, where the people of that Lancashire town, nice as they are, tend to take their pleasures more quietly.

There was a pop group warming up the crowd for our entrance, which we made in a kind of improvised 'Popemobile' supplied by Donnelly Brothers, the local garage. We were preceded by Coalisland Silver Band. I've never known anything so overwhelming – I felt like an American Presidential candidate as I bent down to shake hands with the cheering crowd. As a matter of fact, some joker had actually scrawled 'Dennis for President' on the wall facing our house.

The crowd burst out singing 'He's got the whole world in his hands' as I held up the cup to show them, then they started adding variations on the same tune, like 'He's got Steve Davis all wrapped up in a little black ball'. The car could hardly move for the crowds, who were reaching up and demanding autographs. The sea of people stretched as far as the eye could see. Some were perched precariously on roof-tops. Children kept shouting: 'Dennis, Dennis!' I remembered being a boy like them, walking those same streets in my football boots, past the same old shops: O'Hanlon's, Quinn, Sullivan, O'Donnell, O'Neill, McCrum, Paddy's Bar – and McGlinchey's, where I plead guilty to pinching some sweets. People had gathered from miles away for the occasion – some had even travelled over from Glasgow.

By this time we had managed to reach the platform, where the Lord Mayor was waiting with half a dozen priests, some from as far as Armagh and Tyrone. He made me put on his red cloak. My nieces and nephews climbed up to say hello and sat on our laps. My father and sisters were there. The crowd were chanting and yelling. It was all the most wonderful Irish chaos. Pearse Kelly, from Gervin's club, tried to establish some order and called on the priests to speak in turn.

There was the Rev. Canon McEntegart, Rev. Beamish, Rev. Fr. McKeone, Rev. Fr. McRaois, Rev. Fenton and Rev. Fr. Campbell. Plus Barney Herron, my old headmaster, and presentations from Jim Canning on behalf of the traders of Coalisland, and from the late Jim-Joe Gervin's son, Joe ('the Cowboy') Gervin, on behalf of the grand old club itself. Jim Canning said of me: 'He's brought a bit of life to this town and put us on the map.' I was then presented with a cake in the shape of a snooker table.

I'll summarise the other speeches (I nearly called them sermons) if only to prove I was paying attention. One of the fathers said: 'This is a great day for Coalisland, a day that will never be forgotten. The youngest here in years to come will talk about the day a world champion came back to Coalisland.' Another said: 'What we are seeing around us here today, and what we are celebrating, is life – a life of joy and sorrow. Real life isn't confined to church. We are proud of you, Dennis, a wonderful ambassador for our town and our country.'

The next speaker said: 'Those last few frames were a test not of skill but of character. I was speaking to the Cardinal this morning – he was just off to Lourdes – and he asked to be associated with our celebrations.' This reminded me of a cartoon I saw which showed Prince Charles and Princess Diana leaving the Pope after an audience. Charles was saying to his wife in a puzzled tone: 'He wanted to know if I knew Dennis Taylor.'

One or two more remarks are worth recalling, for this was a special day: 'I've never seen anything that has caught people's imaginations like this,' said a priest, 'even people in hospitals. I saw a woman of ninety-nine in a home who wouldn't go to bed until it was over.' He then asked to touch the trophy – whether to bless it or receive a blessing himself I don't know! Another priest said: 'Thanks for the thrills you gave us on Sunday night, thanks for the joy and happiness that you brought to the streets of Coalisland on Monday morning. Please, please, no more of those nail-biting final frames. It's a great tribute to the people of Coalisland that none of them died of a heart attack that night. I certainly wouldn't have liked to be called out to deliver any last rites while that was going on,' he added somewhat irreverently.

As a matter of fact, I was told that a man did die in Belfast that night – and that, even so, his family couldn't help turning the TV set back on, as soon as they'd laid out his corpse, to catch the final frame. They did this, they told their shocked neighbours afterwards, in the certain knowledge that the deceased would have approved!

I heard of another case in Belfast where a man threw a pot of jam at the wall in his excitement as I sank the final black. At a club the landlord celebrated this same moment by saying to his customers: 'Now you can smash the place up if you like.' I've been told so many stories about that night, things I didn't know were going on, that I no longer know what to believe. But I do know that many prayers were going up for me, and many candles being lit. There was obviously a lot of help.

One visitor from Coalisland was heard to say at a vital moment at the Crucible: 'If he gets this, I'll turn Catholic!' Another visitor – this time a Catholic himself, which 99 per cent of Coalisland people are – had pushed a prayer in my pocket in an interval. Afterwards he asked for it back, because it was very special to him, and offered me a pair of rosary beads instead. He explained: 'Your mother gave me these at my first Communion.' It was his twenty-first birthday that night. So many beads were being rattled back-stage at the Crucible that night, with people running in and out of the dressing-room praying, that the officials didn't know what was going on!

One aspect of my homecoming was especially pleasing. The *Irish Independent* made the point: 'Protestant clergymen in the predominantly Catholic town joined in the victory celebrations, which at one time sounded like a revival meeting. Unlike many sporting celebrations in this country, this one had no political barriers, no religious bias ... and no counter-demonstrations. Only three policemen were on duty.'

Immediately after my victory I had played an exhibition before a large Protestant audience in Belfast's Shankill Leisure Centre, and my reception there had been just as enthusiastic. I know that it will take more than sport to heal the wounds of Ireland, but I am glad that – like my friend Barry McGuigan, the boxing champion – I can offer something in which both communities in Ireland take equal pride and enjoyment.

After the final I received thousands of letters from all sections of the community. One of the most unusual – and not only because it was the smallest – was delivered to my father's front door in Coalisland in the form of what looked like a tiny paper pellet or even a pill. When we unrolled it on the kitchen table it was still only four by two inches in size. It was from H Block at Long Kesh and described how prisoners had banged their cell doors when news of my victory came through. It had been smuggled out of the prison in somebody's tooth!

I should perhaps explain that Coalisland is a strong republican area. The first civil rights march in Northern Ireland had gone from Coalisland to Dungannon in 1968 – two years after I'd left for England. Had I stayed, I suppose I might have been drawn into the politics, like some of the kids I knew at school, but I doubt it. My family have never been directly involved. As a boy I remember the marches of 12 July with the band blazing away. We used to run out into the road and copy the bandsmen twirling their sticks in the air, but it was just fun really. We had no idea what it was all about.

When the troubles started, professional snooker players stayed away from Northern Ireland for a number of years. Graham Miles, then 'Pot Black' champion, was the first to come back. I remember he was playing at one club and I was playing nearby. He came over to my club because there was a big party going on. When he walked up the stairs he got a standing ovation that lasted for six or seven minutes. The band stopped playing and eventually he had to get on the stage and say a few words. It has been like that ever since with all the top players throughout Ireland. There has never been any trouble.

I remember once, though, when Terry Griffiths was playing some trick shots at Gervin's, he announced the 'machine gun' – a trick in which you play the white ball slowly across the table and then fire off as many reds as you can into the same pocket before the white arrives there. (I once potted thirteen reds at this trick, which is some sort of record.) On this occasion Terry said, 'The only trouble is that I haven't got a machine gun' – to which a voice in the audience replied: 'Don't you worry, Terry. We can soon fix that up for you!'

On that same trip I pulled Terry's leg when we passed a tailor's window. 'You don't have to get nervous,' I said, 'just because that dummy over there has a bullet-proof vest on!'

That was 1980, the year I won the Irish title for the first time and a year after Terry had beaten me in the final of the World Championships. It was that match that brought us together as friends. I brought Terry, Steve Davis and Doug Mountjoy to play at Gervin's. Terry and Doug stayed with my mother and Steve with Louis Conlon, the veteran marker at Gervin's, up the road. We all had a marvellous time.

Some people think Steve is stuck up, but he certainly wasn't on this occasion, coming down in his braces for bacon and eggs with the Conlon family. He sent them a box of chocolates afterwards.

I remember that we all had to do a party piece. Doug sang 'Danny Boy' and Steve tried to play the theme from 'The Old Grey Whistle Test' on a mouth organ. This provoked my father to put on a special exhibition to show

15

Steve Davis how to play. How to play the mouth organ, that is: there wasn't much any Taylor could teach him on the snooker table then.

As for Doug Mountjoy, he is always a bit sore that he isn't recognised in the street as easily as some of the other players. Knowing this, I decided to play a little trick on him. I went before him through Customs and asked them to give him a hard time. 'Who are you?' they said when it came to his turn. 'I'm myself, Doug Mountjoy, the snooker player', he said proudly, slightly affronted that they didn't know already. 'Have you any means of identification?' the Customs Officer replied imperturbably. Later in Belfast we were crossing the road to play at the Ulster Hall when the cars started pipping their horns. Doug turned to them with a smile on his face thinking that at last he had been recognised, and gave the cars a regal wave. All they did was honk again – this time more crossly than before – for he was standing in a busy traffic lane!

I came back twice to Coalisland to celebrate becoming world champion – once for the civic reception and once to play snooker at Gervin's. I felt I owed it to the club for all that it had given to me as a boy. I was only sorry that old Jim-Joe Gervin had died some years before he could know what happened to the young lad he stood on a lemonade box and whacked with his feather duster whenever I made a wrong move.

His son, Joe ('the Cowboy') Gervin, has carried on where his father left off. In a town where a dozen people may have the same surname, eleven of them need a nickname to stand out from the rest. I can safely say without exaggeration that I have been in snooker clubs that are more plushy and luxurious than Gervin's, but there is nowhere on this earth where I feel more at home.

First I gave an exhibition for the kids of the town – kids

16

of the age I was myself when I started playing there, some of them even younger. It was more like a noisy children's pantomime than the kind of hushed atmosphere I'm used to now. Anything less like the Crucible would be hard to imagine.

The kids were running around yelling and squealing with pleasure, climbing over seats, having the time of their lives, many of them not even watching the play. They were popping flashbulbs in my face even as I leaned over to play a shot. They cheered every stroke I played and booed my unfortunate opponent.

Despite this crazy atmosphere – perhaps even because of it – I played some good snooker. My concentration didn't seem to be affected at all. I quickly scored a break of 96 and then made one of 112.

In fact, that one might well have been my first maximum break of 147, for I sank fourteen reds and fourteen blacks and the last red jumped out of the pocket with all the colours playable. Even if I'd made it, however, I doubt if it would have been recognised, as there were hardly any adults in the room to witness it!

My series of trick shots went down with these kids like a Paul Daniels magic show. There was no shortage of volunteers for the grand finale, when I get someone to lie on the table with the chalk in his or her mouth. I then pot the black off the chalk into a far pocket. Every trick worked to perfection – which isn't always the case, by a long chalk!

The same lively atmosphere continued for the adult performance. I was genuinely moved by the applause and the shouts and the spontaneous signs of affection. I fill up easily at the best of times, but this was a real tear-jerker, especially with my father and my sisters in the audience. I even counted five priests, which inhibited me a bit in telling some of my jokes!

Despite all this emotion, my glasses cleared long

enough in the first frame for me to make another big break. I even brought up the century cheekily with my left hand and went on to reach 126. 'That's the last time you're getting tea in our house!' said my opponent, Pearse Kelly's brother.

I was in inspired form that night – everything seemed to come off. One of my opponents was Johnny Rea, son of the former Irish champion. I was surprised to see how much grey hair he had got and called him 'the Silver Fox'. 'I got these watching your black balls,' he said. 'I think he's mixing me up with Sammy Davis Junior,' I replied.

When some joker in the audience shouted, 'Come on Alex!' I said: 'Alex Higgins should have been here today, but he was launching a ship in Belfast and they couldn't get him to let go of the bottle!'

When my opponent missed an easy shot and somebody shouted, 'Check the table,' I replied: 'No, I prefer it to be green like it is – we're not playing draughts.'

I can honestly say that I've never enjoyed an evening so much. It was magic. The warmth and friendliness crackled in the air. Everybody wanted my autograph, even though many of them had known me all my life. When I introduced a new award at the club, the Annie Taylor Trophy, the feeling that came back from the audience hit me like a wave in the chest.

Nearly twenty years had passed since I left Coalisland. But if home is where the heart is, that's where I undoubtedly was.

'The key to Dennis Taylor is roots,' a writer once said. He was quite right. Even though I have now lived more than half my life away from Coalisland, it is there that the story has to begin. On 19 January 1949, to be precise. On that same day in other parts of the world Harry Truman was installed as President of the United States and Mao Tse-tung's Communists took over in China. Nearer home, Eire decided to declare itself a Republic and clothes rationing ended in Britain.

But the outside world rarely intruded into the daily life of Coalisland. The little town lived up to its name in those days, with coal and clay mines still providing jobs, but they've been run down since and most people now work in the weaving factories or the pipe works (where I started myself) or try and seek a humble living on the land.

The house I was born in stood by the canal in a row called 'Lineside'. I remember barges used to go by. It must have been very damp there, but my four sisters and two brothers and myself grew up to be healthy enough. There were very few illnesses, which is amazing when you think about it.

There were only three rooms in the house – a living-room where we had our meals and watched television, a bedroom for my mum and dad, and one for all the children. We had to put a curtain up between the boys and girls. Their whole bed collapsed one night.

As we got older, I used to go and stay with Mrs Rush next door and my brother Martin lived with my grandma. It was quite common in those days in Ireland for an older child to live out with relations. In about 1960 we moved up to Mourne Crescent on a new estate, which seemed an enormous place after that, with four bedrooms.

My father drove a lorry for an egg company until it got too much for his bad back. We must have been poor, I suppose, but we were always well dressed and never wanted for anything. I don't know how mum and dad managed that. There were seven of us: me and my two brothers, Martin and Brian, and my four sisters – Brenda, Molly, Jean and Margaret. When those girls are together, it's not easy to get a word in.

My father's people came from Cookstown and may have been Scots originally. Both he and my mother were always devout Catholics. My mother used to go to mass virtually every day. I became an altar boy at St Joseph's at a very early age.

Mrs Rush, our neighbour who was like a second mother to us, used to wake me up for 7.30 Mass and make doorstep chunks of toast and strong tea that I can still taste in my mouth when I think about it. We sat eating it by the fire. Mrs Rush had false teeth but she never wore them because they frightened me.

One of my sisters used to go with me at the start because it was so dark walking by the side of the canal. In those days it was the habit for relations to sit around telling ghost stories in the kitchen, which was more entertaining than television – except for 'Deputy Dog', which was always my favourite. There were lots of stories about the ghosts of dead people appearing at a window or standing by a gravestone, and people used to insist they were true. We kids used to sit there terrified, drinking it all in.

Anyway, these were the sort of things that used to go through your mind as you walked by the canal in the early morning, especially if there was nobody with you. I don't think Sebastian Coe could have got up to the church faster than I did! Once, when I was coming from the pictures, I was sure I'd seen a ghost and arrived home as white as a sheet. When my father came out and looked, we found it was only a bush that had been shaking in the wind.

We had a wire fence round the house and the last one home from mass had to shut the gate. I could never be bothered going all the way round and used to jump over the fence. Once I landed with a bump and ruptured myself and had to go into hospital. I must have enjoyed it there because six weeks later I did the same again!

I was a bit of a daredevil, I suppose, always challenging people to jump over a six-foot concrete-sided river. I was lucky I never fell in. I must have been accident-prone, though, because I hurt myself very badly on another occasion – in fact, they told me in hospital that I had been within an inch of losing my life. There was a travelling fair in Coalisland with some pleasure boats. My mum used to warn me not to go near them. But for some reason we were playing tig around the pleasure boats and I tried to run underneath one. It caught me right on the top of the head. I still have the mark. I lost two of my teeth and had dozens of stitches.

I was very lucky because the boy I was with dived in and pulled me to the ground before it could hit me again. I hadn't been knocked out completely and was trying to stand up. He probably saved my life. His name is Gerry Lyons and he lives now in Accrington.

The two girls in the boat took me to the caravan, where I remember seeing a bucket of blood and thinking, 'That's mine!' They then took me to Dr O'Kane's, where my father came and held my hand until the ambulance arrived. I remember feeling that everything would be OK as long as he was around.

When we got to the hospital a shilling fell out of my pocket and rattled on the floor as I took my jacket off. Even though I was groggy, my father remembers me saying: 'Save that for me. I'll need it for snooker!' I've heard since that the priest was warned that he might be needed for the last rites, but nobody told me at the time.

The only long-term effect was to stop me taking up boxing as seriously as I would have liked, because I found it made me feel sick. It really affected me. I won two schoolboy bouts and was thought to have a promising future. In the second fight I won despite breaking a thumb, so it's perhaps as well for my snooker that I didn't pursue a career in the ring. My sister Brenda remembers me trying to get her to practise boxing with me at home. She would flail me with her little fists while I cried: 'You're not doing it properly!'

My early training in pugilism gave me a special

interest in seeing Barry McGuigan's world title fight against the Puerto Rican holder. I saw Barry after the fight in his dressing-room. Trish and I had a personal escort of twenty policemen down the tunnel. She found it rather frightening. A few weeks before, a reporter had asked me if I had any advice to offer Barry from one Irish champion to another. 'I hope he sinks the black quicker than I could,' I said.

I always had a natural aptitude for sports, especially Gaelic football. I was captain of the Coalisland team when we won the East Tyrone school championship. I'll never forget being carried back through the town on their shoulders after that. So my hero's return after the snooker victory wasn't the first time the town had fêted me – though I have to admit that there were only three or four people on the streets the first time around.

I played for the Tyrone minors team and scored in every match. Then the colleges broke up and some of their players were brought in to our team. Evidently the selectors thought they must be fitter or something. I was fed up at being dropped, so I tried soccer instead and turned out at left-back for Coalisland Celtic.

We were playing against a strong side from Dungannon and trailing 1–0. Then Parley Jackson, one of the team's great characters, slipped the ball back to me. I was about thirty-five yards out, but as a Gaelic footballer I could kick the ball fairly hard. It finished in the corner of the net. I remember that the other players, led by Finbar Burns, who still lives in Mourne Crescent, came racing across the pitch and pinned me to the ground to congratulate me, just as they do in Cup Finals. It's fairly common now, but I'd never come across it before. It was quite an experience, I can tell you, especially for a bashful lad like me.

I kept up the soccer when I moved to Blackburn and played for the paper mill where I was working. One fellow there tried to get me to go to Blackburn Rovers for a trial, but in England the season collided with snooker and I hadn't time for both when I was already working twelve-hour shifts.

I think I made the right decision. Apart from anything else, you can go on much longer at snooker. Look at Fred Davis, who reached the world semi-final at the age of sixty-eight. That gives me another thirty years to think about, please God.

We were a happy family, though I seem to have been a bit rough on my long-suffering family. My sisters complain that I had a nasty habit of firing paper pellets at them from an elastic band until they were black and blue. I used to creep under the curtain in their bedroom on all-fours making noises to frighten them.

My sister Molly was once locked in a neighbour's house. As everybody tried to pacify her, I apparently made funny faces through the window at her and told her she wouldn't get out till Christmas, which of course only made her worse.

Once Brenda and I were accidentally locked in the house when I was nearly two and she was just a baby. People were alarmed to see me climb into her pram and stick bits of paper over Brenda's face.

We once lost a football in a gully and threw stones to try and dislodge it. In the end I threw half a housebrick and hit one of my sisters on the head. I begged them not to tell my mother.

One day I was having a friendly fight in a sandpit – at least I think it was friendly – with my younger brother Brian, who kept annoying me by jumping on my back. I had pinned him to the ground the way boys do, when my father spotted us from his lorry. He stopped and chased me up the street in front of everyone, the toe of his boot just missing my backside by a fraction of an inch as I dodged in front. It must have looked very comical. I was a pretty fast runner at school, but I couldn't get away from him and said ruefully to my sisters afterwards: 'I didn't think Dad could run so fast!'

I also put young Brian, when he was only three or four, on the end of a rope hanging from a tree over a patch of grass. It was a lovers' lane where goats grazed. When I pushed him he fell off and they had to fetch the priest, who gave him sixpence. 'Will they give us another sixpence if I do it again?' I cheekily asked.

I was not just naughty to my own family. There was a girl called Kate Kelly who got excited when she saw some bluebells down a slope and ran home to get some scissors to cut them. I got there first and plucked them all. By the time she returned they'd all gone – and she never knew how or why. Come to think of it, I don't know why I did it either! Like all young boys, I did my share of scrumping, especially cabbages and fruit. I even confessed to the priest once that I'd stolen Teddy Lynch's rhubarb.

I've never been much of a do-it-yourself man, though I tried once to paper Mrs Rush's kitchen. It was a complete disaster, full of patches and bubbles, and looked ridiculous. Later in life I tried to paint a bedroom and Trish was alarmed to wake up at 3 a.m. and see this fellow in glasses crouching on top of the wardrobe!

Another time I was eager for us all to see an eclipse of the sun at 4 a.m. I got my sisters up in the middle of the night and we crept down to watch, but Dad sent us back to bed. We got up again later, but found Dad had taken our bulb out.

At Christmas we would all creep downstairs to see the presents the moment our parents had gone to bed. We'd go around feeling everything in the dark and guessing what the shapes were. We'd even pip horns and make a terrible noise, but they never seemed to hear us – I guess they were absolutely shattered.

I remember one year I got a crocodile leather wallet, my first grown-up present. It wasn't so much the wallet that thrilled me as the ten-shilling note inside. That was a lot of money in those days – and it meant a lot of games of snooker!

I was always terribly shy with visitors and used to sit in the corner and never utter a word. If anyone said anything to me I was likely to burst out crying. I couldn't argue. Even today I steer clear of arguments.

This made it all the funnier when Brenda and I did our party piece for visitors – we used to waltz round the living-room with a dead straight face. We were so serious that people used to burst out laughing and that would then set me off crying! I recall that Brenda and I used to be sent to collect coal in a buggy that my father had made. One of us would get a ride on top on the way there and the other on the way back.

I had a job selling ice-cream at the local cinema, which I did to get some pocket money for snooker. I had to go round at the interval with a tray. I was usually so keen to get back to Gervin's or to football that I just rushed round the place, giving people no time to buy anything at all. Sometimes the manager, Gerry Shields, used to make me go round again very slowly. He often finished up having to sell the ice-cream himself, so he might as well have not had me there really.

Kids used to get up to all sorts of tricks in the picture house while buying the ice-cream in the dark. I had to keep my wits about me. I just had a little light for looking at the change, but you got to know the feel of the money. I remember that ice-lollies were twopence, choc-ices threepence and the tubs were sixpence.

When one little fellow asked me for two choc-ices and a tub I knew that cost a lot and wondered where he'd got the money. He gave me half-a-crown – at least it looked like half-a-crown but it didn't feel like it somehow, so I took a good look at it under the light. It wasn't half-a-crown. It was a penny with silver paper round it. He must have spent hours working at this primitive piece of counterfeiting because the paper was wrapped so tight it might have taken anybody in at first glance. But it was the feel that found him out.

I used to go and help the manager sweep the picture house in the mornings. I hated the job really but the reason I did it was because you'd maybe find a shilling or sixpence that somebody had dropped down the seat in the dark. That was always good for three games of snooker at least.

My secret vice in those days was sweets. I used to hide them from my sisters behind the bed, especially Murraymints which I got from the cinema. They'd ask me for a toffee and I'd say, 'I haven't any, I've eaten the last one.' Then they'd drag me away and pull out the bed and find a whole sweet-shop hidden there.

'Sweets, snooker and chips' is how my sisters remember me then. They underrate me: I was also partial to roast beef and trifle, I remember, and fish and chips and Kennedy's Paris buns, which were like snowballs.

On a more serious note, people have often assumed that the close relationship I developed with my mother was a result of my fame and success on the snooker table. But that's not right. It went back much earlier, even before I was born. I had an elder brother, Thomas, who died at the age of two of meningitis while my mother was expecting me. This nearly broke her heart, so she saw me as some kind of replacement from on high. 'God took one and gave us another,' she used to say. As a result, she always thought of me in this rather special way.

I went to Primate Dixon's Memorial Boys' School, which was where everybody went in Coalisland. I came second out of a class of forty. I got ten out of ten for mental arithmetic and ten out of ten for my handwriting, which has always been very neat. When I went back to the school, Barney Herron, the headmaster, made the point that one of these skills was useful for adding up the score at snooker and the other for signing autographs.

When I was signing an autograph for one little boy at the school, he said: 'Thanks very much, and now you can have mine!' Somebody once gave me a cigarette packet to sign and while I was doing it a hand crept up from the crowd and stole the cigarettes from inside!

One day at school the headmaster didn't turn up and his class was divided up among different classrooms. I went to Miss Kelly, who had taught me when I was younger. I had to go out of the room for some reason while she gave us some arithmetic to do. When I got back I asked my friend Jim Mallagh to give me the answers. Instead of giving me the answers he had worked out for himself, for he was quite good, he gave me any old numbers, with the result that I got the sums all wrong. I felt rather ashamed as Miss Kelly said to me severely: 'I remember, Mr Taylor, when you used to be quite a clever lad!'

I was very pleased recently when the school asked my father to go and talk to the boys, an experience they all greatly enjoyed – none more so than my Dad, who has been thrilled by all the letters he has personally received from fans since my mother's death. It has certainly taken his mind off things.

I always had to sit in the front row of the class at school, just to see the blackboard. In fact, I needed guidance to find the front row! My eyesight was always a problem, especially the left one, and I've only just begun to conquer it in the last few years. But more of that later.

Barney Herron used to write to me in England saying I should treat every defeat as an experience, not a disaster, something I should learn from, like being at school. I was doing my learning in a pretty hard school by then!

There wasn't a great deal to do in Coalisland apart from snooker and betting on the horses. I always preferred the snooker, which I discovered at the age of nine. Louis Conlon still remembers the lemonade box I used to stand on when I began. Even with the rest I had great difficulty reaching across the table. So much so that we used to relax the rules when old Jim-Joe Gervin wasn't about and lie across the table without leaving a foot on the floor.

I'd learned to play with marbles and a wooden spoon on the kitchen table, using upturned cups as pockets. We lost many handles that way. John Spencer also learned to play with marbles, while Steve Davis practised with coloured beads.

It cost a shilling to play and I sometimes had trouble raising it. I'd stand outside Mrs Rush's window trying to catch her eye while she was knitting, without disturbing her husband who would be sitting smoking his pipe. Eventually she'd get fed up with my signalling and come outside and give me a sixpence just to be rid of me.

The loser would usually pay, so I got used to playing for nothing and once cheekily accepted a challenge when I knew my pockets were empty. When it was clear I was going to lose, I pretended to go to the toilet, locked the door and made my escape through the window!

One day the same thing happened to me. John Dillon had challenged me to a single-frame match for half-a-crown. I gave him 40 points start. I set off with a 39 break, the first score of the match. This was too much for him. He put down his cue and fled, leaving me to pay for the table.

It was one of Jim-Joe's fondest sayings that 'You can't break a billiard ball'. Then, much to everyone's amusement, someone hit a ball so hard that it jumped off the table straight into the furnace that heated the room.

Jim-Joe's golden rule was broken – and so was the ball!

To encourage us, Jim-Joe offered five shillings for any snooker break over thirty and any billiards break over fifty. I went to him so often to claim my reward that he finally decided he had to take the notice down or go broke.

I agree with what Ronnie Harper of the *Belfast Telegraph* wrote in a letter to Gervin's after my victory. It was put up on the club notice board. 'The friends one makes in one's youth decide a man's character', he said, 'and Dennis Taylor's outlook on life pays a massive tribute to men like Jim-Joe.'

I was lucky that Jim-Joe had the imagination to allow boys into his club at all. This wasn't common in Ireland. We were allowed in from five-thirty to seven in the evening – mainly so that he could keep us out for the rest of the time! He was a wonderful character, always dressed in a shopkeeper's brown coat, wandering around tapping us with his duster.

He was one of those unconsciously funny people who is forever saying bizarrely memorable things. Everybody has their own favourite Jim-Joe story. I heard him say solemnly once: 'The road to Dungannon is black with white raincoats.' I also heard him say in all seriousness at a club presentation: 'Ladies and gentlemen, I'd like to thank you all, but first of all I'd like to thank myself.' Once, when a black stopped on the edge of a pocket, Jim-Joe muttered: 'Be Jesus, the ball was away there, only it stopped.'

He also had terrible difficulty, as manager of the local football team, in counting the players on to the bus. This was chiefly because there were two brothers O'Neill, which set him a mathematical problem he never seemed able to master. When the bus left without him he ordered another coach. It never occurred to him that a taxi might be enough for one.

I always had a hunch that he couldn't read or write, even though he never let on and always made a great fuss of the bookings sheet for the snooker. But he'd make the players fill it in themselves and when a spare table came up he'd take the sheet to the nearest person and say, 'Now, what's that name written there,' as though the writing was just hard to make out.

I used to sit quietly at the side of the hall holding the rest and rushing forward eagerly to help when a player needed it. I also used to help Jim-Joe put the balls away. I was always hoping I'd be asked for a game. On Sundays Gerry Cullen, the best billiards player in Coalisland, used to practise in Gervin's before the club officially opened. He had a set of keys. I would go knocking on the door until he let me in, then I would set up the balls for him and take them out of the pockets. Eventually he'd say: 'Get your cue out then,' as I knew he would.

Sometimes it was so cold in the mornings, before the heating had been turned on, that Barry Cullen Gerry's cousin, and I, would practise with our gloves on. In fact, I was once caught myself like that in a Christmas handicap match. I came straight in off the street from mass and lost the first frame because my hands hadn't warmed up. My opponent exploited the situation well.

By the time I was fourteen I had come on far enough to play professionals like Jack Rea, the Irish champion, when he put on an exhibition at Gervin's. His wife was from Coalisland and his son still lives there. One night after he'd played me he asked someone how old I was. I was bitterly upset to learn afterwards that he had been told I was sixteen when in fact I was only fourteen. At the time I really imagined that this had blown the big chance of my career.

This was when I hit the headlines for the first time in my life. The *Dungannon Observer* reported: 'Schoolboy Shows Them How in Coalisland Snooker Handicap'. It went on to say: 'A fourteen-year-old schoolboy, Dennis Taylor, is the surprise packet in this year's Geatin's Challenge Cup' (named after the local priest).

By the time I was fifteen I had won both the senior snooker and billiards competitions at Gervin's, against players from Dungannon and East Tyrone. But I was too bashful to carry both trophies home at once and my tiny sister Margaret had to struggle up the street with one of them. I also won the O'Kane Cup and several league medals – the Lido Cup, the Burwat Shield and the Donnelly and Davidson trophies.

My mother never worried about me in the snooker club, because at least she knew where I was. My sisters hated going to fetch me for meals because women were not allowed in and they had to send in a message and hang about until I'd finished a frame. 'Dennis won't come out and we'll catch cold,' they used to complain.

The Coalisland men I played with most at this time were the Cullen family – the brothers Gerry, Ignatius and Plunkett, and their cousin Barry – Peter Campbell (known for some reason as 'Fifi') and Harry Magee. There was also a man called Jimmy Nixon, who used to watch the odd shot and pass on useful tips. I am told he always had faith in me later, even though I wasn't winning anything. I'm glad to see that another Coalisland man, Harry Morgan, now has followed me to England and is shaping up very well. He actually holds the Gervin's club record of 137 against my 135.

We hear a great deal nowadays about coaching at snooker, and some players, like Steve Davis, are obsessed by technique. His father gave him Joe Davis's snooker manual at an early age, and he still goes to a snooker coach at the first hint of a problem with his cueing action. My own experience is that there is no better method of picking the game up than by watching others and learning as you go along.

'Practice makes perfect,' they say – and in no sport is that more true than in snooker – but only if the practice has some point to it. Some players, like Willie Thorne, just practise games all the time, knocking the reds wide open and trying to get maximum breaks.

In my view, this gives you a false sense of confidence, because match-play is never like that. Willie has scored more maximum breaks in practice than anyone else, but never, as he puts it, 'under the cosh'. I stop practising as soon as it bores me. I have to admit that I've never made a maximum break – but so what? I'm still the world champion so I must be doing something right!

I used to play billiards to learn control of the cue-ball, practising going in-off, but I was chiefly a potter of the red ball. There was a canny old billiards player from Portadown called Mills, who had been manager of the Burton's shop. When I was matched against him at Gervin's I was advised to play on a table with tight pockets, but it made no difference. Even though he was nearly seventy, he used so much 'side' on his little pointed cue that the balls still found their way in. I was annihilated.

At the time I started, people still played billiards in the clubs, even though the professional game had died many years before. Now, of course, everybody plays snooker. I was equally good at both at that stage and went on to become British junior billiards champion. But my stocky build and my cue-action were later to mark me out as a more natural player of the 'tomato game', as the old-time pro Tom Reece used to call snooker. People have compared my build and my action to those of the great Joe Davis – who also had trouble seeing out of one of his eyes.

About 1967 we began to hear stories of a wild young genius from the Jampot billiard hall in Belfast who had already won the All-Ireland amateur snooker championship. His name was Alex Higgins, better known as the Hurricane for his speed around the table – and for his fast

Above: *The picture that says it all. Steve and I are both clearly choked by emotion as I win the World Championship and he gives it up. My lenses steam up at the sight of David Vine and the right one assumes the shape of a hot cross bun. Meanwhile, Steve has eyes only for the trophy — or is it for that black he missed in the corner pocket?*

Left: *The hero's return. Back home in Blackburn with sons Damian and Brendan.*

Right: *In Coalisland with mother, Martin, Brenda and thumb-sucking Molly. The top of baby Brian's head is just playable over the cushion in his pram.*

Below: *Mrs Rush, our adopted 'Granny', with Martin, Molly, Brenda and me. She woke me up for mass with doorstep chunks of toast and hot tea.*

Left: *Trying out my new glasses with Martin up-front.*

Below: The Democrat *published this cartoon of me at Jim-Joe Gervin's as a young player.*

Listen here "wee" Dennis! If you can't pot that ball "Jim Joe's" going to have to buy you a "big pair of glasses"!

Praying that I'm facing the right way for the camera on my first holy communion at the age of seven, about a year before I started playing snooker on a lemonade box at Gervin's.

Below: *Trish and I met at a dance in Blackburn in 1968. Here we are at that time (centre) with my aunt Kathleen and uncle Bert (left), my aunt Lucinda and Trish's aunt Teresa (right).*

Top: *Back to Coalisland for a game at Gervin's with Jackie Bates, the Irish billiards champion, and Ignatius Cullen.*

Above: *The British junior billiards champion for 1968 receives his trophy in Birmingham from someone called Clive Everton. I wonder what happened to him?*

Right: *Practising billiards at the Old Post Office Club, Blackburn, 1968, after winning the British junior billiards title.*

Below right: *Wedding day, 1970 — the only possible excuse for the simulated wig and the simpering expression.*

Left: *Joe Davis, 'Mr Snooker' himself. He picked me out in 1974 as 'someone to watch'. He also had trouble with his eyesight!*

Below left: *The bride and groom on the day they lifted the triangle off at St Mary's Roman Catholic Church, Blackburn, on Easter Monday, 1970.*

TOPHAM

TAYLOR FAMILY COLLECTION

Top: *A favourite picture with my favourite women: Trish and my mother at Gervin's in 1975.*

Above: *Young Damian, aged 3, takes his cue from Dad. Note the clever use of the wall. Nowadays he prefers golf.*

living away from it. His potting from all angles was already a legend. He came up to play an exhibition at Gervin's.

He was exactly the same age as me and because we are both from the Six Counties our careers have crossed at many points. Because Alex is a Protestant from the Donegall Road area of Belfast and I am a Catholic from Tyrone, people have assumed that we are naturally opposed on political or religious grounds. It isn't like that at all.

We are not natural buddies because we are different kinds of people, with different interests, temperaments and lifestyles. But we've had some fun together at times and I respect all that Alex has done for snooker over the years. He brought the flamboyance of youth and the spirit of a dashing buccaneer to a game that had come to be associated with middle-aged crinklies in bow-ties and waistcoats. That was just what the game's image needed then to make it attractive to a new generation who were coming to it for the first time through television.

Alex was a sporting folk-hero in the modern mould of another Belfast Protestant, Georgie Best. Both did a great deal to make their sports more popular – and in the process both did a great deal of harm to themselves.

Alex will always be remembered in Coalisland for a match he played at Gervin's in his teens against a fellow called Tommy Walls. Being Alex, he had come over with a crowd of his pals from Belfast and they had all placed heavy bets on him. He was playing so well at that time, potting balls from anywhere, that he became over-confident. Tommy Walls played such a steady safety game that Alex was completely frozen out. All he could do was complain about the pockets. He finally stormed out of the club with his mates without even paying for the table!

It must have been about this time that Alex took a shine to my sister Molly, who used to help make the tea at Gervin's. You couldn't really blame him, I suppose, for she has always been strikingly pretty. But knowing Alex's reputation with the girls I wasn't too keen on this relationship and came on a bit strong with the older brother bit.

I needn't have worried, however, because Molly was perfectly capable of looking after herself – and even if she wasn't, our mother certainly was. Alex told Molly he'd buy her an engagement ring if she'd go out with him for a month. Then he came up to the house and told my mother: 'If I can't marry Molly, I shan't marry anyone.' Molly was hiding under the stairs by this time, pretending she was out.

Finally, when Molly said she couldn't see him because she had a boy-friend, Alex replied: 'I can't fight him myself, but I have friends in Belfast who'll make him a cripple.' To be fair, he later apologised for this remark and sent a note up to the house. Alex is very good at apologising, but then he's had plenty of practice.

He was so determined to press his suit with Molly, however, that when we all took him to the airport he deliberately carried little Margaret, the youngest, out on to the tarmac on his shoulders so that he could give her a letter for Molly. He told her not to tell anyone but Molly about this, but when we got in the car Margaret blurted out: 'Look what Alex gave me!' As my mother's hand reached out for the *billet doux*, all hope vanished of a lasting liaison between the Higgins and Taylor families.

I became a keen dancer in my teens. At that time the craze was for jiving, for which I wore skin-tight jeans. My sisters used to get me to bend over while they stitched them up and I'd pay them sixpence to polish my shoes.

This was in the days before discos. We had record hops

instead. But there were also visiting live bands and groups that came to Coalisland, like Joe Dolan and the Drifters. I'd sometimes help out in the cloakroom. I remember the Bachelors coming. Once I got the autograph of their lead singer, Con Cluskey, and held on to the ballpoint pen for years, thinking it belonged to him, which it probably didn't anyway. I little imagined that I would one day sign autographs myself.

As a matter of fact, though, I did sign some autographs even then. I'd sometimes help the bands to set up their stuff and carry the instruments for them. Then, at the end of the evening, I'd sit at the drums and tap about while the band were having a drink or talking to the fans. Then people would come up and ask for my autograph, thinking I was part of the group. I'd just scribble something on a piece of paper.

I had a pal called Francis Quinn and we fancied ourselves at the twist. One day we saw that a twist competition had been advertised in Dungannon, about four miles away, so we decided to enter for it. But his mother wouldn't let him go out in mid-week. We were so keen we worked out a plan to get him there.

He lived near the school in a house that backed on to fields, so he changed in his bedroom, sneaked out of a back window – and off we went to Dungannon. When we got there, we found the dance had been cancelled anyway! It never occurred to us to think how his mother would have felt if she had gone to his bedroom and found him missing.

Most of the time we walked the four miles to Dungannon and we'd think nothing of it. If we were lucky and had some money left, we'd maybe grab a taxi. Often there would only be the one, so a dozen people would each pay a shilling and pile in. I once counted fifteen people in a single taxi. You'd have no chance in an accident.

Sometimes there would be a late bus back to

Coalisland. I remember being with this friend Jim Mallagh, who now lives in Oxford, outside a dance-hall when we saw the last bus moving off. We were out in the middle of nowhere, so we raced after it.

All we could see was a ladder at the back, which led up to the roof of the single-decker. It was probably used to put luggage on top. Jim grabbed at it and climbed up, then I just dived and hung on to the rail because the bus was going like the clappers.

Eventually, when we'd scrambled up on top in the dark, it suddenly dawned on us that we were coming to a part of the road where the trees would overhang the bus. We remembered from being inside the bus on other occasions that branches would rattle on the top.

Then we saw a tarpaulin and crawled under it just in time, as the trees scratched away at our backs. But at least we weren't knocked off into the hedge at the side of the road in the middle of the night.

When we reached Coalisland the bus stopped outside a café. Two policemen waiting there were astonished to see us coming out from under the tarpaulin and climbing down the ladder. Before they could recover from their shock, we had raced off up the street.

At dances in Ireland the girls all lined up on one side of the room and the fellows on the other side. You'd pick one out who looked OK from a distance and go up and ask her to dance. This was all very well for most of the chaps, but I had this problem with my eyesight.

I'd spot a girl who seemed to look all right, then I'd walk over and as I got nearer I'd see I was making a dreadful mistake. I'd end up asking the girl next to her, no matter what she looked like, or having one embarrassing dance, then dumping the poor girl. But I'm glad I stuck to the dancing, because that was how I eventually met Trish, my future wife.

By this time I had left school and taken a job at the pipe works in Coalisland, looking after the kilns. My father had wanted me to become an electrician, but I took this job because some of my mates were there. Eight of us were eventually sacked because a faulty batch of pipes had got through. The manager, Mr Harris, later offered me my job back, because he realised I wasn't to blame. But he'd already done me a favour by sacking me, I realise now, because that forced me to think about going to England, which I then decided to do.

For a shy boy of seventeen who loved the closeness of family life, it was a serious step to take. I knew there'd be times when I'd feel homesick – for the family, Gervin's and for Coalisland itself – but, like many generations of Irishmen before me, I had no real alternative. The boat from Belfast to Heysham was a frightful experience. What I didn't know at the time was that the move would revolutionise my snooker. I didn't even pack a cue to take with me on my adventure across the Irish Sea.

PART TWO

A Lancashire Lad (1966-72)

It was a vintage year, 1966. England won the World Cup. Harold Wilson won a General Election for Labour. The Swinging Sixties were in full flow, with the Beatles at their peak and the girls in shorter mini-skirts than my mother would ever have allowed my sisters to wear back home in Ireland. America announced a plan to put the first man on the moon. Meanwhile, back on earth, the only giant step for mankind that really affected me was the one over my Aunt Sheila's threshold at Darwen, near the Lancashire mill town of Blackburn, for this was to be my home for the next few years.

John Pulman fended off the challenge of Fred Davis for what passed as the world snooker championship in those days. It had virtually died as a major sporting event since the late 1950s. Not that I had much interest in such matters then. I hadn't brought a cue over from Ireland with me because I had gone to England to work.

Besides, I imagined that the level of play on the mainland would be much too sophisticated for a young lad from Gervin's who had never played outside the area where he lived. My highest snooker break before I left Ireland had been 54.

When I went along for a game to the Old Post Office

Club in Blackburn, I thought the players would be far too good for me. But I found to my surprise that I was at least as good as the best amateurs playing there. So I decided that I'd better go out and buy myself a new cue with one of my first wage packets.

I remember that wage packet very well. It contained £26, including five fivers. I went into the gents to count it. I had got a job cutting out patterns for the carpets in cars – the kind of cars, Jaguars and Mercedes, that I never imagined I'd ever be rich enough to own. One day I cut myself so badly that my little finger was nearly severed. I gave up the job immediately because of the risk to my snooker.

The purchase of that snooker cue had proved to be a good investment. I made a remarkable improvement with it, and within a few months I had made my first century break. What I had happened upon by accident was nothing less than the hot spot of snooker, for the part of East Lancashire that included Blackburn and Accrington turned out to be one of the most competitive areas in the country. This was the second piece of luck I had had in my snooker career – the first being born within walking distance of Gervin's.

I played in the Blackburn snooker league. Although I enjoyed the team matches and gained from the experience, I often felt it was a wasted night, since you ended up playing only one frame. For most of the team it was just a good night out with your pals while you had a few drinks. But I was teetotal then, so I didn't have that pleasure. I felt I would be better off practising.

My next piece of luck was meeting John Spencer, who was then just reaching his peak. He went on to win the first of his World Championships in 1969, ending John Pulman's long run. One of the local papers launched a Find a Champion competition, which started with Spencer playing exhibitions against young hopefuls, the best of whom were selected for further matches.

Jim Meadowcroft and I soon joined this circuit and found ourselves matched against the cream of the Northern amateurs. It was the best possible apprenticeship in the competitive game and my play soon started catching some local headlines. 'Drill Hall Crowd Rise to Brilliant Taylor', 'Sparkling Show by Taylor', 'Brilliant Taylor Hits Top Form' – these yellowing cuttings all date from that period.

I went on to win the Accrington and District singles title and the Champion of Champions event. Whenever John Spencer played an exhibition against a team of local amateurs he invariably found me the hardest to beat, and it wasn't long before I was taking frames away from him. John was always one of my strongest backers long before I turned professional, and I readily acknowledge a personal debt to one of the nicest men in the game. 'Cueman', the columnist in the *Lancashire Evening Telegraph*, wrote around this time: 'Spencer has long had a high opinion of Taylor's ability ... he told me Dennis would one day win a major tournament and then there would be no stopping him.'

It is hard to exaggerate the importance of this kind of encouragement when you are just starting out. My uncle had now got me a job in Waterside paper mill, working twelve-hour shifts operating a machine, so I needed every bit of encouragement to keep me going at the snooker table in the evenings.

'Cueman' was the pen-name of John Taylor, who did a great deal for snooker in Blackburn. He was also an A-class referee. I'm glad for this chance to repay the many tributes he paid to me in print in these formative years, when a young player could so easily have been put off by negative comments. There is a great contrast between these old provincial journalists, who really know the game, and some of the lads from the nationals who are sent up these days to sniff out scandals (real or imagined) without knowing one end of the cue from the other.

One of 'Cueman's' pieces was picked up and quoted in *The Democrat* back home – possibly prompted by my mother, I dare say. Under the heading, 'Coalisland Boy Makes His Mark in England', it read:

A little time ago I saw a young Blackburn player in action and was most impressed by his play. Last week Dennis Taylor, the player concerned, confirmed my high opinion of him when he gave British champion John Spencer a real trouncing in an exhibition game. The way he went about it was a treat to watch.

Dennis tells me he is also a keen billiards player with many good breaks to his credit. Last week he sent in his entry for the British championship. There are some who think he is reaching too high in such a quest.

I had entered for this almost as an afterthought. But I proved those people wrong and that I wasn't reaching too high at all when I won the British junior billiards championship in 1968, beating D. Burgess of Portsmouth by 684 points to 536 in the final at Edgbaston in Birmingham. In the final I made a personal best break of 130.

The trophy was presented by Clive Everton, now editor of *Snooker Scene* and generally acknowledged to be the leading writer and historian of the game. Clive had won the same title himself in 1956 and was later four times runner-up for the English amateur billiards championship. Other names on the junior billiards trophy were those of Rex Williams and Mark Wildman, who are still among the stars of the three-ball game. Willie Thorne was to take it three times after me and Steve Davis won it in 1976.

41

I had been put out of the junior snooker championship in the final of the Lancashire section by Geoffrey Peacock, from Manchester, who beat me 3-2. He made 57 in the deciding frame, which was a big break in those days. I never won the amateur snooker title, which was generally regarded as the passport to a professional career, chiefly because it was so hard to get past my keen Lancashire rivals. Doug French of Liverpool, who later turned pro and has now reverted to being an amateur, was often a problem for me in those early days.

Even so, I had made progress, as the *Lancashire Evening Telegraph* confirmed.

There can be no doubt that 1968 was a great year for Lancashire snooker, with three players producing really outstanding performances to give the Red Rose County something to shout about.

First there was David Taylor's world and English amateur championship wins; then Dennis Taylor's junior billiards championship; and, on the professional scene, John Spencer's victory over the reigning world champion, John Pulman.

'Cueman' went on to select me as his Player of the Year for 1968. 'It was Taylor's great performance against John Spencer at Darwen last month when, with breaks of 50, 60 and 70-plus in consecutive games, he trounced the professional star 3-0 that swayed me to the Darwen youngster,' he said. 'That was the finest exhibition of amateur or professional snooker I have seen in many years following the game.'

Then came the summer, when it was traditional in those days to take a break from the game. 'You try to keep interested,' I told a local reporter, 'but it's difficult when the sun is shining outside.' I used to play a few games to keep my hand in at the Old Post Office Club (later called the Benarth) in Blackburn with David Briggs and Arthur Bradshaw, and also put in some hours of practice at the Central Conservative Club.

'It will mean sacrificing some other pleasures,' I told the reporter, 'but I intend making an effort to get on in the game. You have to keep at this game if you want to be consistent, and the better your opponents the better you play. Snooker is the game I prefer really, but I find billiards helps my snooker a lot. It's a good way to master control of the cue ball.'

I had given up my shift-work at the paper mill because it had become too exhausting. My brother Martin had to wake me up in the mornings when my Aunt Sheila was out at mass, and he found it increasingly hard to dig me out of bed after my late nights in the snooker halls. I was in need of a rest.

I'd saved up some money, so I went back to Ireland for several months. I played some good matches back at Coalisland and Dungannon with Alex Higgins and with Jackie Bates and Maurice Gill, two Northern Ireland champions.

My friends back home were clearly impressed at the progress I'd made. *The Democrat* wrote this about a billiards match I played against Jackie Bates: 'For the next nine minutes we concentrated solely on the fair-haired Coalisland cueist. Dennis played solo for nine minutes during which he compiled a truly brilliant 110 break, which included several difficult shots – necessary because lady luck was not always on his side. The audience gave a great round of applause when the break ended. The modest cueist blushed.'

I had reason to be modest, for Jackie went on to beat me by two points. Alex, who was by this time All-Ireland amateur snooker champion, also beat me 3-2 in a snooker exhibition that night, but I was pleased enough with my form. *The Democrat* headlined its report: 'Snooker and

Billiards at its Best'.

The Dungannon snooker columnist, 'Baulkline', wasn't so impressed though. He said sternly of Alex: 'Higgins has a long way to go before he will be a match for the professionals or, for that matter, many of the top English amateurs that are about these days.' Within four years Alex had made a devastating response to 'Baulkline' by winning the world professional title at his first attempt.

I remember Alex at these matches talking to me non-stop, even while the others played at the table. He had already been drawn to the North of England after winning a team tournament at Bolton for the Belfast YMCA. A local promoter had then taken him up and arranged some exhibitions. He wanted to hear more about the life I was leading in Blackburn and the level of snooker there. The upshot was that he eventually came over and settled in Blackburn himself. I helped him to find a flat.

Looking back, 1968 was a magical year for me. Not only was I British junior billiards champion, but I had won golden opinions in Lancashire snooker and had scored a victory over John Spencer, a world professional champion. I even got a new job when I came back from Ireland – as weighbridge clerk for Reid's, a transport company that operated out of the Darwen paper mill. They gave me the job because of my neat handwriting. Then something even more magical happened: I met Trish!

Her aunt and mine knew each other in Blackburn. We were both from Catholic families. My aunt Sheila had her sisters Kathleen, Peggy and Lucinda staying in the house before they got married. (Peggy was later to die in a car crash on a visit to Ireland.) My brother Martin and I had been spoilt at home because our sisters had always tidied up after us, but in Darwen we had to learn to hang up our own clothes. I won't say the aunts indulged in any matchmaking exactly, but they certainly arranged for us to meet. Trish came over to the house one night to do somebody's hair – she was a hairdresser – and stayed with us chatting and telling jokes until about one o'clock in the morning.

I badly wanted to take her home. I had a battered old Standard 10 car with its own ventilation system – a hole in the floor. But I was so tongue-tied I couldn't get round to asking her. In the end my uncle drove her home.

A few weeks later there was a Battle of Britain dance at King George's Hall in Blackburn and the aunts arranged for us to go together. They told Trish I was a good dancer and wanted to meet somebody to go dancing with. When I asked her to jive, though, it was a bit of a disaster because she danced the English way and I danced the Irish way.

Somehow we stayed on the floor together, neither thinking the other was much of a dancer, until the last waltz – I remember it was an Engelbert Humperdinck record. We went home together in a taxi. Even then I was too shy to ask her out again. My brother Martin bumped into Trish's Aunt Teresa and said I'd like to take her to the pictures.

Trish remembers that I just sat quietly in the cinema all evening holding hands – that's the way we did things back in Ireland. She also remembers that the first time I ever declared my feelings I couldn't find the words and wrote 'I love you' with a finger on the steamed-up windscreen of the car.

One benefit of my bashfulness was that we did not go in for many lovers' tiffs. I can never stand arguments anyway, even now. But we had a humdinger of a row once in the street, which stands out in the memory because it was such a rarity. We had been to church for confession on a Saturday night and the argument started on the way back.

It got very heated, so I walked down one side of the road

and Trish walked down the other. We came to a point where there was a bridge and one side of the road was much higher than the other. I suddenly realised I was holding her handbag, which I had grabbed during the argument, so I hurled it blindly across the road. It landed right on top of her head and nearly split it open. I was then in a panic because I thought I had killed her. Anyway, it ended the argument.

Trish had a boy-friend at the time, but he had three disadvantages compared with our hero – he couldn't dance, he didn't have a car and he didn't have a quaint Irish accent. So he stood no chance.

We used to go over to Manchester sometimes to meet some old friends from Coalisland: Gus and Peter Quinn, Vincent McCusker, Laurence Lyons and Oliver O'Neill. Trish made trifles which became famous and we used to drive over with them wobbling on her knee. The car doors were held together with bits of rope. I sold it eventually for £7.50, including two freshly re-moulded tyres.

Seeing how some of my old friends were living made me realise that this was what it would have been like for me in digs if I hadn't been staying with my aunts – queueing up for the cooker with my eggs and bacon in the morning. I don't think I could have stood it for long. I was homesick enough, but at least I was with my own people.

Trish and I were married at St Mary's Roman Catholic Church in Blackburn on Easter Monday, 1970. We were both twenty-one. We went to St Bee's in the Lake District for our honeymoon, but we had to come back after three days because we'd run out of money. Trish and I were thinking of this recently when we saw honeymoon couples at Limassol in Cyprus who must have spent at least £3,000 on a honeymoon.

By this time I had joined Relayvision, a television rental firm. The sales director who gave me the job, Eric Parks, is now a manager with Riley's, the snooker table manufacturers. I went from working inside the shop to being a representative with my own Morris Minor van.

I became a man of property with a terraced house in Blackburn, which we bought for £950. But it had an outside toilet, I recall, which used to embarrass me. So I tried extending the kitchen area with the help of my uncle, but I had terrible trouble papering the extension because it was slanted. I got the paper up with my hand but every time the whole thing just fell off and we dissolved in laughter.

Although I was playing a great deal of snooker by this time, we never really imagined that I would make a living at the game. Trish used to come and collect me at the Old Post Office Club, where I'd go to practise in the evening.

Because I was playing my snooker so locally – concentrating on matches in Blackburn and Accrington with the occasional excursion to Preston, Burnley or Blackpool – the people back in Ireland thought I must have disappeared from the face of the earth. Louis Conlon, the old Gervin's marker, recently found a cutting from a Dungannon paper of 1970 which is headlined: 'Dennis Taylor, the Forgotten Man in Snooker'.

The paper reports my mother going to see me play for the first time while she and my father were on holiday. As luck would have it, I was playing Higgins in an exhibition match which he won by six games to three. Asked how she had enjoyed it, she was quoted in the paper as saying: 'It was great. Young Higgins was terrific. In fact, he had the crowd laughing their heads off!' She evidently didn't understand that crowds weren't supposed to do that at snooker matches!

Interestingly, the same paper mentions my younger brother Brian, then fifteen, who had reached the semi-final of the Gervin's Youth Cup and the quarter-final of the Father Geatens Memorial Cup (both of which I had won at his age). The paper says Brian's style is not like mine, however – but 'very reminiscent of Alex Higgins, with lots of accurate potting and no real safety play'.

The year Trish and I were married I won the East Lancashire snooker championship, which caused some fuss in the local Press because it was the first time the title had ever come to Blackburn. I beat Tony Sowden of Accrington by four frames to one. 'Cueman' was ecstatic:

In this final I saw East Lancashire snooker grow up, if not to maturity, at least to a standard near international level.

No matter which way one looks at it, it was a great final. That Tony Sowden ran up a 60 break, yet finished a 4-1 loser, tells the story of its brilliance. By cutting out all the needless safety play and going courageously for their shots, both players made it far more entertaining.

In that respect Taylor and Sowden did a good job for local snooker. But what really made the match was the 'standing room only' crowd which turned up in support.

And what a select crowd it was. I could have made up an all-star team to take on the best in Britain from those present. Also there were many stars of years gone by among them, and as we talked together one and all were full of enthusiasm for what they had seen.

There are many snooker fans who think this East Lancashire win is the breakthrough needed by Taylor to put him on the road to better things to come.

Another commentator referred to my 'ice-cool temperament', which helped to make me 'the master of any situation. His control of the white ball is now almost legendary among amateur snooker players in the area.'

Someone else noted the new enthusiasm for snooker at

this time among the paying public, which had been boosted perhaps by the success of 'Pot Black' on the BBC. 'In a night, it seems,' he said, 'officials, players, promoters and spectators have suddenly discovered this is a sport with great potential. When the experience sinks in,' he added prophetically, 'we can expect that enthusiasm to explode.'

By this time 'Cueman' was describing Jim Meadowcroft and myself as 'the two best Northern amateurs' as we travelled round the clubs on the Find a Champion circuit. We didn't just visit snooker clubs either. As 'Cueman' says, 'Our stars don't spend all their time pot-hunting. There are times when they play snooker for the enjoyment of it.' We played at the YMCA and for the old-age pensioners – 'Both players thrilled the pensioners with 80-plus breaks.'

I went on to win the East Lancashire title four times in five years. One of these defences – against George Comberbach – was described as 'the best show in the history of the championship'. George Comberbach was one of the top amateurs in the area and practised a lot at the English Electricity Social Club. He had read Joe Davis's snooker manual and used to pass on some useful tips.

I was then chosen to represent the England amateur team against Wales and Scotland, which was a great honour, even if I still felt very Irish. I had just met the residential qualification by living in England three years.

My selection was prompted by a world amateur record break of 136 – a total clearance – that I made against Jim Heaton, the Lancashire champion, at the Huntsman Hotel in Blackpool. He split the reds but it was the only shot he got as I despatched every ball on the table. This break must have knocked me out, though, because I promptly lost the final four frames and the match. I was very disappointed when this record was not officially ratified, on the grounds that it had not been made during a major championship. There was quite a fuss about this, and rightly so, since we were playing in a four-man competition on a match table with a grade A referee. To say it didn't count was like saying Roger Bannister's four-minute mile shouldn't have counted because it was not in the right competition. They gave me a certificate to say I had made the break – which I knew already – but they refused to call it a record.

The title I really wanted – and the one everybody expected me to get – was Lancashire amateur champion. My best chance came in 1971 when I went 5-1 up overnight against Dennis Hughes of Manchester at the Cob Wall club in Blackburn and needed only one more frame for the match. It seemed to be a formality when I resumed the next evening.

But it all went wrong as Hughes won all five remaining frames. I couldn't hold the cue at all. 'Cueman' was beside himself. 'How Taylor came to lose that championship will still be a major talking-point in years to come. The question most people are asking is: why did Taylor change his tactics from the attacking game that had given him a 5-1 lead on Monday to miserable defence on Tuesday?

'There have been many inquests on his failure and the reasons for it. In the majority of cases the verdict was temperament. My verdict is that Taylor committed championship suicide by changing his tactics. He should have gone for the kill when he had Hughes on his knees crying for help.'

The story behind my shock defeat was both simpler and stranger than that. On the second evening I had just come straight from the hospital in Blackburn, where Trish had just given birth to our daughter Denise. Every time I bent to play a shot my eyes started brimming over and all I could see was the baby!

Because I had been expected to have an easy victory that night, Alex Higgins had been asked along to play an exhibition with me afterwards, so that the customers wouldn't be disappointed. But the final went on so long it was after midnight before Alex came on, and he had grown visibly fed up about the delay. He had wanted to be showing off earlier. I then added insult to injury by making a century break against him. 'That's the baby's birthday present,' I said. I'd opened up the reds for him, but he missed and let me in. Because the match was over I'd suddenly lost all the tension. I could destroy Higgins but I couldn't win a frame against the other bloke.

It showed that there was nothing wrong with my snooker – that it was baby Denise who had unknowingly come between me and the cup. No prizes for guessing which mattered more to me. Damian, our next, was born while I was playing an exhibition against John Spencer, but I don't recall that it affected my play.

By this time Alex had moved to Blackburn, where I fitted him up with a Relayvision TV set. We practised together at the Old Post Office Club and played 'sticks', three-handed money matches, with Jim Meadowcroft. Alex has claimed that he took a lot of money from us, but my recollection is different.

Alex was now a professional and heading towards the big time. Ronnie Harper of the *Belfast Telegraph* said of him at this period of his life: 'Gone is Alex's cheeky little boy attitude. He's now a player dedicated to his job, a job that could see him take his place among the great names of British snooker.' His manager in Blackburn, John McLaughlin, had made him the talk of the snooker circuit.

It was around this time that I began to see the benefits of good management. I had taken over the Find a Champion circuit from John Spencer and played a number of exhibitions with Doug French. On one occasion I remember he got fifty pence – out of which he had to pay his own bus fare! After one match at Troy Street Pensioners' Club, I remember, Spencer had been given twenty cigarettes after an exhibition. I got a box of chocolates because I didn't smoke! They used to make tea right by the table as we were playing. A few years later I was very touched when the pensioners sent me a letter enclosing £2 to help me go to Australia.

I was helped greatly by Ben Clarkson, who owned the Elite Club in Accrington and had become secretary of the East Lancashire Association. He brought considerable organisational skills to this job and improved the quality of snooker in the area. The Elite Club that year won five out of the six county trophies – the only one they missed being the final I lost to Dennis Hughes on the day Denise was born.

But Jim Meadowcroft, Steve Longworth and I helped the Elite to the Lancashire club championship, thanks to a final frame clincher by yours truly, which was some consolation for the other defeat. 'A tremendous cheer greeted Taylor's win,' said the *Accrington Observer*. 'It kept up his record of victory in every round of the championship.'

In 1972 Alex Higgins made his dramatic breakthrough, shaking the professional game from top to bottom with his victory over John Spencer in the World Championship at Selly Oak British Legion in Birmingham. After that the game was never the same again. My game had got closer to his, whittling down the 21 start he used to give me. I had also beaten Spencer. I had a wife and daughter to support. It was time for me to reach a decision on my future.

When I won the East Lancashire crown again, there was much speculation that I might turn professional. 'Cueman' wrote:

You just can't keep Dennis Taylor out of the news these days. If he isn't beating the amateurs, he's knocking professionals about, and on Wednesday he put up what must rate as the best performance of his exciting career.

Playing on level terms, he beat the ex-Irish champion Jack Rea 7-0 at Hollins Grove Conservative Club, Darwen. With performances like that to his credit, is it any wonder that talk of his turning professional goes around?

This time there is some basis for presuming that Dennis might do so. The facts are that strong influences are working overtime trying to persuade Dennis to venture into professionalism, and substantial financial backing is there for him should he decide to make the changeover. I know Dennis is seriously considering the propositions put to him, but he is a sensible enough man not to be rushed into making any rash decisions.

The 'strong influences' he was referring to meant Ben Clarkson, who offered me a job as manager of the Elite Club he owned in Preston. It was a tempting offer, because it not only guaranteed a living wage but, even more important, ample time for practising snooker.

Besides, Trish was still earning good money as a hairdresser. In fact, she was already earning more than I was with the TV rental company – and she was to continue earning more than me for my first few years as a pro. Without that to fall back on, I might not have made the plunge. We certainly couldn't have managed on my earnings from snooker alone.

I was also influenced by a chat I had with a fellow called Brian Slater, who was managing a shop for Riley's. He now has his own company called Allied Billiards. I used to go to his shop to get tips and glue for my cue and various bits and pieces. He convinced me that the professional game was about to take off.

It was partly a result of 'Pot Black', which had been a phenomenal success with the public. Promoters and sponsors were showing interest in reviving the World Championship on a knock-out basis with sixteen professionals. At that time there were still very few professionals, so it seemed a good moment to try.

It was a big step to take. I thought I might be applying too early, because I hadn't won the English amateur title, which was the usual stepping-stone to the professional ranks. It was a relatively slim amateur record on paper. So I didn't know if I would be accepted or not. But I put my application in and John Spencer spoke up for me. That must have helped a lot, because none of the other top players – Pulman, Reardon, Fred Davis, Rex Williams – had ever seen me play at that stage.

That was the fourth piece of luck in my career. The first was Gervin's, the second coming to Blackburn, and the third meeting Spencer. The fourth was turning pro at just the right time in the history of the game.

PART THREE
Pot Luck (1972-79)

People have often asked me how snooker got its unusual name. It used to be thought that it derived from a certain Captain Snooker in the Indian Army. Unfortunately that isn't correct, but the bit about India is true enough. The game originated in the officers' mess of the Indian Army at Jubbulpore in the nineteenth century.

The soldiers grew bored with billiards, which only two can play, and tried some variations, using many coloured balls so that more of them could join in, especially during the rainy season. The coloured balls already existed because they were used by Indian princes at traditional games like 'Slosh' and 'Pyramids'. 'Life Pool' and 'Pink Pool', which were chiefly gambling games, also needed coloured balls. The scoreboard in my snooker room at Blackburn is an old 'Life Pool' marker.

One day in 1875 (according to the writer Compton Mackenzie) when the Devonshire Regiment were stationed at Jubbulpore, a young subaltern arrived straight from the Royal Military Academy at Woolwich. He told them that a 'snooker' was a jokey term of abuse for a raw young Army recruit.

Later, when the man was playing at the table, he missed a simple shot and an officer called Neville

Chamberlain (no relation of the Prime Minister of that name) called out: 'You snooker!' In later life Chamberlain told Compton Mackenzie: 'I had to explain to the company the definition of the word, and to soothe the feelings of the culprit I added that we were all, so to speak, snookers at the game, so it would be very appropriate to call the game Snooker. And so it has been ever since.'

Billiards, of course, is a much older game, probably deriving from France, where Louis XIV, the Sun King, had a table at Versailles. The French usually played without pockets, relying on cannons. Mary Queen of Scots had a table at Fotheringay Castle, where she was executed and carried out on it, and in Shakespeare Cleopatra proposes a game of billiards.

In the last century and in the first half of this one billiards was regarded as the real test of skill, whereas snooker was looked down on a bit as a working-class game for gamblers. Billiards reached a peak in those week-long challenge matches of the 1920s and '30s at Thurston's, near Leicester Square, when Joe Davis and Sidney Smith played the Australian Walter Lindrum.

In fact, they became so good – especially Lindrum, who once compiled a break of over 4,000 points – that the public got bored with it. The non-striker would sit for hours on end in his chair – sometimes for days – while his opponent amassed a huge break. Joe Davis used to say his trousers went shiny while he was waiting for a shot. It can be hard enough sitting out at snooker, but at least the suffering comes to an end after one frame.

In the old days of billiards, before the rules were changed, a man called Tom Reece trapped the balls in the jaws of the pocket and played cannons for a week. At one 'point he turned cheekily to his opponent and asked: 'What kind of chalk do you use?' Then he said to the referee: 'You should ask this man to pay for admission'.

Just as public interest in professional billiards died, so snooker took its place. This was chiefly the work of Joe Davis, who won the first world professional snooker championship in 1927 and reigned supreme until he retired undefeated from tournament play in 1946.

Then his younger brother Fred – who, many people say, had more natural talent but less dedication than Joe – kept the title in the family for another ten years. It is ironic that yet another world champion called Davis should have come along now, but Steve is no relation.

Just as professional snooker seemed to have taken over where billiards left off, it too suddenly went into decline. That was in the mid-1950s. The main reason was the introduction of television to the family home, which kept people out of the clubs.

There was so little interest in the World Championship that it wasn't held at all between 1957 and 1964. Even when it was re-established, it was just a challenge match against the reigning champion in which there was little public interest or excitement.

Just as the withdrawal of Walter Lindrum from tournament play in the mid-1930s had effectively killed off interest in professional billiards, so the withdrawal of Joe Davis a decade later seemed to have killed off professional snooker.

It was certainly true that snooker became a bit of a closed shop, with Joe Davis deciding who could be admitted to the professional ranks. He excluded anybody who didn't meet his own high ideals of what a professional snooker player should be like.

As a result, a number of gifted amateurs, including money players like Patsy Houlihan who beat Spencer for the UK amateur title in 1965, couldn't gain admission to the magic circle. Rex Williams was the only new professional for about fifteen years. The public got tired of the same old faces. When Joe Davis finally retired in

1964 he was asked about the future of the game. 'What future?' he replied. 'Professional snooker has no future.'

'Pot Black' made all the difference when it was shown on colour TV in 1969. Snooker suddenly took off again as the public were fascinated by the colours and the subtle complexities of the game. The cameras seemed to invade the players' innermost thoughts, showing all the tension on their faces. And the whole arena could be comfortably contained within the TV screen.

This new boost to the game owed a great deal to Ted Lowe, known as 'The Voice of Snooker' because of his TV commentaries, who had been manager of Leicester Square Hall, the great temple of snooker in London. When it closed in 1955 he worked hard to stimulate new commercial interest in the game, and it was he who finally persuaded the BBC to give it another try.

Earlier experiments in black and white hadn't been much of a success, though it is fascinating now to see old film of Joe Davis. He was playing with heavier balls in those days and the pockets were smaller, so there was less long potting than there is with modern players. But he used side, stun and screw for position exactly as they are played today.

It is strange to think that just as it was television that nearly destroyed snooker by taking people away from the clubs, it was also television that brought it back to life by stimulating a new public interest, even among thousands of people who had never played the game.

It was fortunate that 'Pot Black' coincided with the arrival of a new generation of professionals. John Pulman and Fred Davis gradually gave way to the likes of the Welshman Ray Reardon and my old friend John Spencer, who had pleasing personalities for the television screen. The battles between young and old were to entrance the nation's viewers.

And then, of course, there was the Hurricane, who

swept away the old image of the game at a stroke with his dashing victory over Spencer in 1972. He undoubtedly attracted a totally new audience. Whether some of that audience are what the game really needs is more doubtful, especially when they behave like parts of the crowd at Wembley last year. Nonetheless, for all his faults, Alex Higgins' major contribution to professional snooker cannot be denied.

This was the brave new world into which I tiptoed at the end of 1972. I was a poor boy from Northern Ireland whose only experience of the wider world had been the dour, smoke-filled snooker halls of a remote corner of Lancashire. I hadn't been to London more than once or twice, and then only as a tourist. I peered out at this new world through my glasses and wondered what I had let myself in for.

It started all right – in fact, with a bit of a bang. 'Taylor Gets Off to a Flying Start,' said the local paper. 'Blackburn's snooker star Dennis Taylor got his career as a professional away to a flying start with a 5-2 victory over world champion Alex 'Hurricane' Higgins. Playing before a packed holiday crowd at Waddington Social Club, Clitheroe, both the champion and Taylor produced some excellent match snooker.'

I repeated this win over the reigning world champion in the replay on my home patch at Highfield Working Men's Club, Darwen. This time I did even better, winning by a margin of five frames to one, which was doubly satisfying after Alex had bragged to the local press: 'I'll whip Taylor 5-0.' According to the same paper, I played some of my finest snooker that night. 'Hurricane Shattered by Taylor' was the gratifying headline.

My winning streak continued on a return visit to Belfast. Ronnie Harper of the *Belfast Telegraph* commented:

Dennis Taylor brought a breath of fresh air into the Belfast set-up. A young player with a great future ahead of him, he was the essence of consistency. It's been a long time since Belfast fans saw a professional with so much to offer. He averaged a 50-break in each frame of the many he played.

Taylor, too, delighted the crowd with some trick shots. He showed just why he has a full snooker exhibition calendar in England. Like all professionals, he made the game look very easy. A prolific screwer of a ball, Dennis thrilled the crowd with his accurate potting and tracking in a match which could herald the return of big-time snooker to Belfast.

All this time I was working alternate weeks in the Preston snooker club and trying to set up matches and exhibitions for my week off. Ronnie Harper's talk of my 'full English snooker exhibition calendar' was a bit exaggerated. The money I was getting was far from princely – £17 or £18 for a night's exhibition was about average. My records show that I got £38.25 for one engagement in Brixton – and I'd have paid my own expenses out of that.

The snooker club left me plenty of time for practice in the mornings and afternoons, but there was always a rush of customers at lunchtime and early evening. I could tell that the game was gaining in popularity because people like sales representatives started coming in to play in the afternoons as well.

Sometimes I would get bored in the club and enjoyed any distractions. More than once I beat a prospective hustler who had come swanking into the club looking for easy game. I had a weighted cue-ball which I sometimes swapped with the real one, especially where I thought the lads would enjoy the joke. But there was some rough stuff as well. I once had to warn off a huge man who kept lying on the table and I was afraid he would damage the cloth.

When I switched off the table light to remonstrate with him, he threatened to hurl me down a sixty-foot well outside.

Managing a snooker club in Preston had its drawbacks, especially the hours, from nine in the morning until eleven at night. Many a night I would drive the ten miles home and just get into bed when the police would ring to say the alarm had gone off. I would have to go racing back from Blackburn, sometimes with the whole family sleeping in the back of the car. We eventually discovered that the alarm was being triggered by a mouse running up the TV aerial. This was somehow catching on a metal pie tray which activated the beam. I lost many a night's sleep over that.

The only real tournament in those days was the World Championship. There wasn't a whole circuit as there is now. That was your one big chance of the year – and your earnings for the rest of the time would be greatly affected by your performance there. That would establish the demand for your services at exhibitions and invitation tournaments, and that would set the price you could ask. Trish used to conduct these negotiations for me on the telephone and arrange my diary.

You can imagine my feelings when I went out in the first round of my first World Championship in 1973. I lost 9-8 to Cliff Thorburn, the Canadian grinder, in what could be described as a real 'cliff-hanger' – the first of many I was to have with the genial Canadian champion. I had seen Thorburn for the first time at an exhibition in Blackpool, where he was having trouble adjusting to British tables. The Canadian pockets are easier than ours.

But he had made the adjustment by the time I played him in Manchester. As ever, my old friend Cueman was there to see the game: 'I'm sure Thorburn must have counted himself a very lucky man to be still there after

61

his clash with Dennis Taylor. The Canadian won in the seventeenth deciding frame after having had more than his fair share of luck in almost every frame of the match.'

Even allowing for Cueman's natural Blackburn bias, he was quite right. But I had only myself to blame, as he showed. 'In seven of the games he lost, Taylor had Thorburn trailing forty or more points in arrears, yet failed to press home that advantage and allowed the Canadian to wriggle off the hook far too often. Nevertheless, it was a brilliant and exciting match, the best of the round, and well worthy of its place on the number one table.'

The tournament itself, sponsored by Park Drive and staged in Manchester's Exhibition Halls, was regarded as a big success – 'the best thing that ever happened to snooker,' according to Cueman. There were more than 25,000 spectators. Thorburn, whose first appearance this was at a British tournament, was equally enthusiastic. 'Ship this show over to the States and you'd make a million,' he said. 'Pounds or dollars?' he was asked. 'Both' was his curt reply.

It was the first attempt to telescope the championship into a fortnight, like Wimbledon, and the first time it had all been brought under one roof. The later stages of the final were televised for the first time. It is astonishing, looking back, to realise that for Higgins' victory over Spencer the year before – a game that revolutionised the whole history of snooker – no TV cameras were present at all. There were hardly any journalists either.

Ray Reardon staged two great recovery acts to win the title. In his semi-final against Spencer he came back from 12-19 down to win 23-22, and in the final against Australian Eddie Charlton he came back from 0-7 down to win 38-22. Both players had been blinded for a while by the television lights, to which they were unaccustomed. I noticed that the pressure brought the best out of

Reardon, who actually seemed to thrive on the tension and the atmosphere of a big occasion. I was used to tough competitive matches, but I clearly still had something to learn about coping with the stresses of a big event.

But I had some consolation by playing in the plate event (for losers in the first and second rounds) against John Pulman, who had held the World Championship eight times. This was the biggest thing in my career up to that point, and I remember that my father came over to watch. I was leading 6-2 when John started getting annoyed with the crowd – he could be very temperamental, having been brought up in the hushed (not to say somnolent) atmosphere at Leicester Square Hall.

Anyway, this put me off my game and he drew level – though to be fair I should add that he played absolutely fantastic snooker and made two century breaks and a 95. My Dad was so excited that I was doing so well against Pulman – who was a giant to his generation – that his eyes brimmed over with tears. He'd seen me beat Higgins, even Spencer, but Pulman was something special, a figure from snooker's golden age. It's astonishing to think that John was put out of the World Championship of 1948 by Clark McConachy, the New Zealander, whose playing days went back to the 1920s and who had competed in the world billiards final against Joe Davis and Walter Lindrum in the 1930s.

Unfortunately, John beat me in the final frame and went on to win the plate from Cliff Thorburn, who had been eliminated in the second round of the tournament 16-15 by Rex Williams. I remember my old man saying to me: 'That has got to be one of the best experiences you have ever had, playing against a player like John Pulman and losing by only one frame.'

John Spencer was always a great practical joker and I remember one he pulled on Pulman. When Pulman went out of the room, he put some super-glue under his whisky glass and stuck it to the counter. Pulman couldn't understand what had happened as he sat struggling on his bar stool, trying to pick it up, not saying anything because he thought he might just have had too much to drink. It was hilarious.

Pulman had clearly passed his tournament peak by this time, but he had one or two more arrows in his quiver. He reached the final of the Norwich Union Open at the Piccadilly Hotel in London and was leading 6-2 before allowing Spencer to level at 7-7. Then he missed a vital green in the final frame. Pulman also gave Spencer a tough fight in the world semi-final of 1977.

After my flop in my first World Championship, it was back to the common round of the snooker pro – now with two children to support – struggling to make a living. I remember driving a thousand miles in a week to cover a series of exhibition matches on the East Coast – to Pontin's holiday camp, Great Yarmouth, Lowestoft and Comber Sands. I did 400 miles in a single day. I was so shattered when I left Lowestoft that I had to park in a lay-by to sleep. I remember waking up and thinking I was still driving, which was a frightening experience.

John Peachey, who ran newspaper and sports shops in Ipswich, had offered me my expenses plus £30 to play my first exhibition in the area. He and his wife Betty became close friends and supporters, and I felt greatly honoured when he invited me to join the board of his company, Canon Sports.

In those days it was very important to get home after an exhibition, if only to save on hotel charges. Arnold Sedgwick used to come with me and share the driving, so that we could get home the same night. He was an expert on cars and saved me from a number of expensive mistakes, including a dolled-up Austin 1100, which seemed a bargain at £175 but would have been a disaster.

David Briggs, who managed the Elite Club in Preston,

used to race me home in his car to Darwen and get me off to evening jobs. I practised with him a good deal. He was a left-hander with as much ability as many pros, but couldn't reproduce it in matches. This happens to a lot of players.

There were so many great characters in the snooker world to whom I was indebted at this time. What generally happened was that you got in touch with someone in a particular area and asked them to set up some matches. More often than not, they got nothing out of it themselves except your company for a meal afterwards (for which they usually paid) and the satisfaction of having brought some good snooker to their part of the world.

Bob Bailey, a manager of Riley's in Scotland, was one of these people. He used to bring Joe Davis north of the border in the old days. I remember sitting with him having dinner off Princes Street in Edinburgh one night when we watched in fascination as a drunk staggered down the road. Because of the slope he was puzzled as to how to get round the corner. He thought about it for nearly half an hour and finally waited for a man to come by, then clutched on to him. It worked – and we all fell about in amusement and admiration.

There was Peter Gray in Aberdeen, an old pal of Ray Reardon and Bill Werbeniuk, who could put on five shows at £20 each, a fortune for those days. On one trip the driver was breathalysed and I was left to drive the huge van to Dundee with a snooker cue in the back. I was shattered and wanted to get to bed. But when I got to the spare room I found the bed occupied by a snarling little dog. Evidently Bill Werbeniuk, a frequent visitor, allowed it to sleep there. I couldn't stand it and finally squeezed it out of the door.

Over at Eastbourne, John Hughes has a small shed which takes thirty or forty people. All the pros have been there. I played a few games there once with Graham Miles. We decided to amuse the audience by dressing up as women, putting on make-up in the bedrooms and shoving apples up our dresses. When we had made up, Graham said: 'I don't believe it, but I look just like my mother!' We were introduced as lady players, but we were rumbled when one of the apples fell out. I immediately tried to pot it.

In Pontypool a policeman called Keith Williams used to arrange some games for me. After the snooker one night we went to a Chinese restaurant, which agreed to stay open only because they knew him. At 2.30 a.m. roused by the crispy noodles, Keith challenged me to a game of squash at Pontypool Leisure Centre. At 3 a.m. the match duly took place, if it can be called that. I hardly saw a ball. That was one night I didn't get home – and I've never picked up a squash racket since.

When people talk about the glamour of a snooker professional's life, they tend to forget those long nights in motor cars, racing to beat sleep and get home to bed to avoid a hotel bill that would swallow up the evening's takings. Or the standing around on draughty railway platforms, which is how Alex Higgins, as a non-driver, has spent much of his professional life.

In the 1974 World Championship I fared even worse – I went out 8-1 in the qualifying round to Marcus Owen, who had just turned professional after winning the amateur title four times. That was very depressing at the time. I began to pick up only when I saw that he was in remarkable form and might have beaten anyone. Had he beaten Reardon in a close match in the quarter-final he might have gone all the way, for Ray went on to win very easily.

Still, that was two years gone as a professional and I had achieved very little. I cheered myself up with a convincing win over Graham Miles, the runner-up in the

World Championship, and found myself placed number thirteen in the professional rankings. Whether that would bring good or bad luck I had yet to see.

But I was touched when the legendary Joe Davis singled me out after the championships as someone whose play had impressed him. As one paper said, 'Coming from the great Joe Davis, the compliment was a happy ending for Dennis in 1974.'

In fact, however, 1974 was far from finished as far as I was concerned. I packed up the job at the snooker club to go the whole hog at the professional game. I had £200 in the bank and two children. It was time I did something. I decided to have a crack at the Canadian Open.

I had to pay my own way out there and saved money by staying for three weeks with Terry Haddock, the promoter, at his house in Toronto. He was the moving force in Canadian snooker and a friend of Thorburn, Werbeniuk and Kirk Stevens. It was the first time I had seen Kirk, who was a flamboyant player.

Even saving on the expenses like this, I calculated that I would need to reach the semi-final to break even.

In a sense that Canadian trip, which had seemed such a risk at the time, turned out to be the making of me as a professional, the breakthrough I had been looking for. I beat Higgins 8-6 in the semi-final. What pleased me about that was that he had beaten me 140-0 in one frame and I came straight back to beat him 138-0, then my highest break, in the next to reach the final. It was one of those magic moments and the crowd loved it.

I lost to Thorburn by the same margin in the final. He was rapidly becoming my bogey man, having already eliminated me in the first round of my first World Championship. Even now I regard him as the toughest man to beat on the circuit. He has that priceless gift – which Reardon also has, and I have now begun to develop myself – of being able to win frames even when he is not on top form. He takes his time, admittedly, but he has always played the game that way and he is not going to start rushing round the table just to please television viewers.

Cliff is one of my favourite people. He comes over serious on television, but then he was brought up in a hard school in Canada, where snooker was a serious game with a great deal of money at stake. In real life he isn't at all serious – in fact, he is one of the game's great funny men, with a deliciously dry sense of humour. I remember being with him in a lift in Bombay once when he had me in agonies of laughter.

But I wasn't laughing too much when he beat me at the Canadian National Exhibition Centre in Toronto for the £1,500 first prize. It might sound crazy, but I swear that a bottle of Coke cost me victory that day. During the interval I fancied a light drink and had to queue up for it. When I got back an official said: 'You're keeping people waiting.'

I know it's ridiculous, but that remark upset me. I let it worry me. I didn't like the idea of keeping people waiting, and I didn't like being ticked off by an official. Until then I had been well in front, yet that tiny thing put me off and I lost. It broke my concentration. I swore never to let such a thing happen to me again.

Because I had been staying on my own at a private house, I had plenty of time to go down and practise all day on the match table. Before the final I was playing against the Montreal champion and broke a world record by scoring 349 points without missing a single shot. This consisted of a 103 clearance, a 134 total clearance after fluking a red from the break-off, then 112 on my first visit to the table in the following frame. I actually scored 24 century breaks during the fortnight in Canada, six of them over 130. This again caught the venerable eye of Joe Davis, who said I was a 'player to watch'.

Even more important than that, however, the BBC

decided I was 'a player to watch' – and included me in their 1975 'Pot Black' series. My gamble in going to Canada had really paid off. Ironically, it was at a 'Pot Black' occasion that I saw Joe Davis play a live shot for the first time in my life. But that was just for the cameras as we all lined up behind the tables, so I was in no position to judge his form with a snooker cue. In any event, he was well into his seventies by then.

I also remember meeting his brother Fred for the first time when I turned up to record 'Pot Black'. He had just come down from finishing a game when I bumped into him, so I introduced myself. We chatted away for about ten minutes before he went to his dressing-room, making me feel very welcome. It was a kind thing for a man like Fred Davis to do for a new professional and I've always remembered it.

Fred always had a genial twinkle, which made him a popular figure on 'Pot Black'. He was once playing a game at a holiday camp when a chimpanzee, which had escaped from the zoo, jumped on to the table. Fred looked at it in surprise, then said: 'Is this my opponent? I don't know all these new professionals.'

Fred had his World Championship match in 1973 interrupted by rain pouring through the roof. He also had the surprising experience of knocking the cue-ball off the table and seeing it land in somebody's glass of Guinness. On another occasion it landed in the fire. That reminds me of the time I played Alex Higgins at an old age pensioners' club on a very bad table. At one point Alex got a wicked glint in his eye and started deliberately knocking balls off the table and landing them in the laps of the startled old folk in the front row.

The importance of 'Pot Black' to a young pro like me was incalculable. It was not so much the money, which was not a great deal in those days. But it meant that my face was immediately recognised wherever I went, thus increasing my appeal to clubs seeking players for exhibitions. It also helped that I reached the final in the first two series of 'Pot Black' in which I appeared, losing first to Graham Miles and then to John Spencer.

Curiously, I got into the 'Pot Black' team at the expense of Cliff Thorburn, who had actually beaten me in Canada, and Jack Rea, the Irish champion. My first 'Pot Black' opponent was John Pulman, whom I beat 98-19 in what Cueman described as 'an impressive performance'.

Alex Higgins also got in that year. He has had a chequered career on 'Pot Black', as in so much else, and was cold-shouldered for a time by the BBC for complaining about being kept waiting and threatening to walk out.

'Pot Black' is so popular now that it's hard to believe they had a problem in the early days finding a studio audience to watch the programme. They had to get the canteen staff and cleaning ladies to fill the empty seats at the Gosta Green cinema in Birmingham. Now the luxurious studio at Pebble Mill holds three hundred people and they have a waiting-list of ten thousand.

The 'sudden death' format of this event – a single frame for the preliminaries and three frames for the final – doesn't suit everybody. In fact, it can be very frustrating to go out of the whole series after hardly playing a shot. It certainly wouldn't do for every tournament to be like this. But the players have come to accept that it's right for this particular TV slot – and those who don't like it are not compelled to join! In practice, the invitations are keenly sought after.

The introduction of Junior Pot Black is a wonderful showpiece for young players. I wish it had existed when I was starting out. Dean Reynolds, a left-hander from Grimsby, won the first Junior Pot Black and has since gone on to the professional game. John Parrott, who won the trophy in 1982 and 1983, has the poise of a future world champion. Neal Foulds is another good player who came up by this route.

Alex Higgins got his revenge on me after the Canadian Open by beating me 5-1 in the Norwich Union Open. I had had to qualify for the tournament by defeating David Taylor, 'the Silver Fox'. In those days half the battle was getting into a tournament, never mind winning it. This one was actually won by John Spencer in a tight finish against Ray Reardon. Spencer's famous old cue had been smashed into four pieces before the tournament in a car crash and was lovingly restored with thirteen plugs and a wood graft by Cliff Curtis of Riley Burwat to enable him to play. The cue was a terrible old thing anyway, even before it was smashed. It had a six-inch nail holding it together. I don't know how he ever played with it.

Eventually John had to give it up and tried one of the new two-part cues to win his last world title in 1977. But there are people who say he was never the same player after that old cue was broken. It's a matter of confidence really.

Old Clark McConachy, the New Zealander who beat Pulman after the war, once gave his favourite cue away to a girl and never dared to ask for it back. Joe Davis says he was never the same player after that. Sidney Smith had his favourite cue, known as his 'pit prop' because it was so short, smashed in his dressing-room by a Sydney gambling mob who feared that he might beat Walter Lindrum. He never recovered either.

Joe Davis thought his career was over when his cue was stolen at Victoria Station, but it was handed in to the police a few days later in Tooting. Alex Higgins has had terrible trouble with his cues ever since his favourite, the one with which he won the world title in 1972, was trodden on by a hotel porter.

I've never been quite so neurotic myself over cues, but I have to admit that my game improved dramatically a few years ago when I tried one a couple of inches longer than what I was used to. It was actually two parts of a three-part half-butt that Del Simmons had arranged to be specially made. Most players like ash, but I prefer a wood without a grain because it's less likely to warp, and currently use a Canadian maple.

The two-part cues are easier to carry around, especially as cabin luggage on aeroplanes, and you feel less like a Mafia hit-man than you do with the long ones in their gun-cases. I remember being stopped by police at Jersey airport who seemed to think I was importing a rifle. I also remember travelling on buses with the long cue in my early days. You had to sit at the back and hold the cue straight up in the air. More than once a short-sighted old lady would grab it, thinking it was the bus rail. On one occasion, I recall, an old dear landed in my lap.

My next target was Australia, where Eddie Charlton had arranged to take the 1975 World Championship. Unfortunately, expenses were being paid for only six invited players and I wasn't included among them, so I had to raise the money from somewhere. Frank Harrop, a Darwen snooker fan, to whom I had given some coaching, gave me a great deal of help at this time by setting up a fund-raising appeal. He was the one who wrote recommending me to 'Pot Black'. I recently came across one of the circulars he sent out:

Dear Sir,
    DENNIS TAYLOR – Blackburn Professional Snooker Star
    At the end of the 1974/75 Snooker Season, during April 1975, the World Professional Snooker Championships are to be staged in Australia, and Dennis Taylor, as one of the World's leading young Professionals, will be competing, endeavouring to become the 1975 World Professional Snooker Champion.

It is a matter of record and regret that the Australian sponsors have not offered any financial assistance to the majority of the British Professionals and therefore, in order, privately, to meet the enormous cost of the journey, estimated at £800, we are currently arranging Dennis Taylor's busiest season, which we know will give him constant match practice together with meeting the huge financial requirement.

We would be pleased if you would support Dennis Taylor's efforts by engaging him to make a personal appearance at your club, which as you know will be fully appreciated by the snooker members. It will also 'pep-up' the league players during the season by simply observing such an expert at work.

He will challenge seven club members conceding a total of 200 points and offer his fee of £25 as prize money if he loses, to ensure a 'money match' interest. He will also offer a £5 prize to any member who makes a break of 45 points or more whilst playing against him.

This outstanding value for money offer is presently being supported and we would be delighted to receive a firm date fixing a match from your goodselves to assist this splendid cause. We will confirm the date, if it is open, by return of post. Please offer two alternative dates.

A publicity poster 18" × 23" will be sent to the club when a date has been arranged.

We take this opportunity of thanking you in anticipation of your kind support, knowing that a thoroughly entertaining evening will be enjoyed by all.

Yours sincerely,
F.W. HARROP
The Dennis Taylor World Professional Snooker Championship Fund Raising Organiser

This was a time of hope for me, as this bullish story

from the *Accrington Observer* of March 1975 – under the heading 'Dennis Taylor is now Making the Breaks' – clearly demonstrates:

The rise of Dennis Taylor as a snooker professional has amazed many, stunned some but shocked only a few. Accrington fans have watched him over the last seven or eight years go from strength to strength as an amateur, turn pro and climb the ladder to snooker stardom.

'Since I have been appearing on "Pot Black", wherever I have played from Newcastle to Bristol the houses have been packed,' said Dennis.

Speaking at the Elite Billiard and Snooker Hall in Accrington he told me: 'During the last six months my play has rapidly improved and in recent weeks I have beaten Graham Miles twice and Alex Higgins.'

Dennis is not loud-mouthed, big-headed or off-hand with spectators. That's one reason for his success. Everywhere he plays he is asked about a return booking.

At Darwen, Dennis staged his biggest coup so far when in front of about 300 excited fans he won eight out of ten frames against that other Irishman who plays from Accrington, Alex Higgins. Dennis made the highest break of the night, an 84, but most of all the match showed just how much he has improved in the last 12 months.

Last year when he played John Spencer at the Drill Hall Dennis himself admits he was second-rate, but his performance against Higgins emphasised he is now one of the top half-dozen snooker players in the world.

During the next few weeks Dennis is concentrating on preparing for the World Championships in Australia. He flies out to Australia along with several other players on 6 April. They stop over in Singapore to play in a small tournament before eventually landing in Australia.

On Tuesday, Dennis plays John Spencer in the semi-finals of the Ashton Court Invitation Tournament in Bristol and the winner meets Higgins in the final.

Another secret of Dennis's sudden surge to success has been the behind-the-scenes work of local businessman Mr Frank Harrop.

'Frank has been a great help to me,' said Dennis. 'He arranged for me to play in clubs throughout the North to raise the fare to Australia and it has kept me in constant practice because it has meant I have been playing four and five nights a week in front of packed houses.

'Playing so regularly has made me more confident when I go to the table. The tension is still there at the start of a match but I think that is a good thing, for when that goes you are probably underestimating your opponent,' he said.

Dennis's biggest fans are his wife Tricia, daughter Denise (4) and son Damian (2).

'I always try to get back home the same night wherever I am playing,' said Dennis, 'but that might be a bit difficult when I am in Australia!'

Even if Dennis fails to win the World Championship – and he is going with the sole intention of bringing the title back to East Lancashire – he can justifiably claim the title held by Spencer: 'The First Gentleman of Snooker'.

I won that little event in Bristol to record my first tournament victory since turning professional. They invited eight players to Ashton Court, now the Redwood Lodge and Country Club, and guaranteed £50 appearance money. In the same final Spencer was 60 up in the deciding frame but I made 62 to beat him on the black.

For the final, I remember, the winner got £500 and the loser £100. It was tempting to strike a deal beforehand at £250 each and the winner to take the extra £100, but Alex was so confident that he didn't want to know. As it turned out, I beat Alex and also won £50 for the highest break, so I got £550 and he only got £100.

The money came in handy because we had just moved to a three-bedroom bungalow at Mellor. I was also trying to raise the fare to Australia.

Frank Harrop's fund-raising scheme worked out very well. He teamed up with Michael Murray of Matthew Brown's, a Northern brewery, who organised a series of exhibitions. The effect was to draw big crowds to the clubs and to make my name better known – except in one of the clubs, where the referee insisted on calling me 'Mr Brown' in honour of the brewery. I can think of several players who deserve to be named after a brewery, but I'm not one of them!

We ended up at Hollins Grove Conservative Club in Darwen, where I was presented with a cheque for £320. That topped up the amount I needed for Australia. It may not sound a fortune by today's standards, when the world champion picks up a prize of two hundred times that amount, but I can assure you that I folded that cheque into my wallet that night with a heartfelt sense of gratitude. (I was also deeply touched by a tenner that was sent to me after a whip-round at an old folks' home.) The arrangement with the brewery was such a success that it went on for over eleven years.

I was beginning to look forward to the Australia trip and told the *Lancashire Evening Telegraph*: 'I fancy my chances. I can do it if I play as well as I have been doing this last six months.' 'Taylor is Confident', the paper said. I gave an extended interview in which it is clear that I saw myself on the fringe of greatness:

There's almost an apology in the air when Mr Nice Guy of the world of professional snooker tells you: 'I'm building up the one thing I've always lacked – the killer instinct!'

Ever since Dennis Taylor came over from Ireland to Darwen, people have admired his charm, demeanour and excellence on the snooker table. But he tells you now: 'You can be the nicest guy in all the world, but if you keep coming second you have to brainwash yourself!'

There is no doubt in the minds of the Spencers, the Reardons, the Davises of the snooker world that Taylor has the potential to be as good as any of them. He knows this himself.

'It's a question of breaking through,' he tells you. What he means is cracking into what might be termed 'The Magic Circle' of professional snooker. 'I know I have to go. I know I'm good enough and I believe I can win the World Championship,' he says.

It's part of Dennis Taylor's make-up that he has a soft spot for the fellow countryman that everyone else – apart from the spectators – seem to dislike, one Alexander 'Hurricane' Higgins. If Higgins is oil, Taylor is water. Chalk and cheese, call it what you will.

They are totally different in temperament. And yet Dennis Taylor will tell you: 'I look at what people can do – professionally. We know Higgins is a bit of a case, but he's a great snooker player – perhaps as good as any the world has seen.

'Normal human beings would drop down dead if they tried to live like Higgins – if they stretched themselves to that degree. Yet if he tried to change at all, if he stopped to think, he'd no longer be Higgins. The beauty of Higgins is he's magnificently ignorant. He doesn't know what the hell he's doing – yet when he goes to that snooker table he makes magic happen.

'I can't be a Hurricane Higgins. It's not in my nature to be that way. But what I can do is beat him, or anybody else, at a moment in time – given the opportunity.'

Dennis Taylor is in that fascinating period of life which you might loosely term the half-way house. He's only twenty-five. The innate ability is there and he has on his side not so much softness as temperament. As he says, he's got a new-found killer instinct.

In other words, which he won't tell you because of his modesty, he now knows you have to do a bit of fighting as well as putting on exhibition stuff.

He grins: 'Believe it or not I've got a green velvet dress-suit on order, with waistcoat and yellow shirt!'

All he has to do now is to get to Australia to try to win the World Championship.

To cut a long story short, I did get to Australia but I didn't become world champion – that was to take another ten years. But I got nearer than I had ever been before, losing to Eddie Charlton in the semi-final. While I was practising in the City Tattersalls Club in Sydney I met Paula Squires, widow of the Australian player Norman Squires, and she offered to put up myself and another competitor in a caravan in the garden of her father's home. She and her father had travelled the world as a circus act, and Paula herself was a good snooker player.

Losing the final to Reardon was a big disappointment for Eddie, who had set his heart on winning the world title in front of his own people. It's hard to explain what Charlton means to Australians. You can go anywhere and mention his name and everybody knows who he is. In a sense, his name is bigger than snooker over there. He is one of their all-time sporting greats, having triumphed at soccer, surfing, speed roller-skating, cricket, athletics, boxing and tennis. He carried the Olympic torch at

Melbourne in 1956.

The World Championship of 1975 was an Eddie Charlton spectacular. Not only was he Australia's leading player, but he was chairman of the Professional Association, ran a promotions company that helped to stage the tournament, and had a major interest in the tables and in the television rights. To have beaten him would have been a kind of treason after all that!

To get the chance of beating him I first had to eliminate Perrie Mans of South Africa and Gary Owen, which I did with frame scores of 16-13 and 23-14. My problem then was a choppy flight from Sydney to Brisbane, from which I hardly had time to recover before going out to play. Eddie, meanwhile, had stayed in Brisbane and played on the same table where he had won his previous matches. He went into an early lead which I was never able to pull back, going down 19-12.

Even so, I'd reached the world semi-final. I felt I had arrived. This was officially acknowledged when I was listed ninth in the world rankings. Unfortunately for me, this turned out to be one over the eight, since it was usually only the top eight players who automatically qualified for major tournaments.

Eddie was playing well, with his famous gun-barrel cueing action, and was hard to beat on his own table. He doesn't use much side, preferring to make sure of the pot. John Pulman says Eddie is 'the only player who *pretends* to put side on the ball!'

His final with Ray Reardon was a ding-dong affair that fluctuated amazingly. Reardon led 16-8, Charlton led 29-23, Reardon led 30-29 until Reardon clinched the championship 31-30 in the final frame. Eddie was never to come so near to the title again. It was the closest result in the final until Steve Davis and I got together at the Crucible a decade later.

Eddie's misfortune was to meet Reardon at his peak.

Ray won the world title for four years in succession from 1973 to 1976, and then came back for more again in 1978. Only Steve Davis in 1981 has matched that consistent form in my experience. I had the misfortune to be in his path in the 1976 World Championship. He mowed me down 15-2 in the quarter-final.

Ray has been a great ambassador for the game. Everyone was delighted about his MBE. He is a very cool customer under pressure, as he showed when he was a coal miner and was buried under a roof fall for six hours – he played frames of snooker in his head so that he wouldn't move and bring the whole lot down on him. Then he was a policeman and dropped in on a burglar through the roof.

And he looks the part, too, with his neatly brushed black hair and his immaculate turn-out. Mind you, if you'd seen him in his dressing-room just five minutes before, he'd have looked rather less dignified, standing around in his underwear. He rushes into his evening clothes at the last possible moment. He is fondly known on the circuit as the Welsh Dracula – I make jokes about this in the commentary box sometimes, like 'Reardon pots the red and draws first blood.'

You have to watch his little mannerisms if you don't want to be put off. Once he was playing Big Bill Werbeniuk in a morning session, a time of day Ray never likes. He's a man for the big occasion and likes the formality of the evening. When Bill missed a shot and walked away from the table, Ray said: 'I can see you don't like playing in the mornings either, Bill!' Bill couldn't pot a ball after that. He shouldn't have let it bother him, but somehow it did and the old Welsh wizard had pulled off another master-stroke.

In the 1976 World Championship Ray saw me off with some pinpoint snooker, the best I've seen him play. It was a curious tournament that year, a bit of a disaster in many ways. It was played partly in Manchester and partly in Middlesbrough. The promoter, Maurice Hayes, disappeared – he was later reported to be driving a taxi in Canada.

He had really big ideas about snooker and he introduced Embassy to the event, so he deserves to be remembered in the history of the game. He saw the potential. His problem was organisation. He had no back-up. He'd make verbal arrangements with people and never confirm them in writing, then he'd forget all about them. In the end it must have got too much for him to catch up with, and he flipped.

In 1977 Mike Watterson took over as promoter of the World Championship and moved the event to the Crucible Theatre in Sheffield. His wife had seen a play performed there and thought it had the right intimate atmosphere for snooker. She was quite right. It was an inspired move. It's a bit like a church, with the hushed congregation looking down at the altar as we all go about our priest-like tasks. You also get a very nice mix of people in the audience – without the noisier elements that are unfortunately creeping in elsewhere.

The move to the Crucible seemed to suit me. Apart from anything else, it wasn't too far from home across the Pennines. I reached the semi-final for the second time, going out to (guess who?) my old sparring partner Cliff Thorburn. It was another of our tough matches, 18-16. Cliff is rightly known as the Grinder on the circuit. He uses every bit of his ring craft and experience, slowing the game down or speeding it up as it suits him.

Cliff once played non-stop for fifty-four hours against a gambler called Canadian Dick in San Francisco. 'He came in with a jar of speed pills to stay awake,' says Cliff. 'But I really knew he had come to play when he laid out three pairs of socks! Our needle matches over the years have never been quite so long – they just seemed like that!'

Cliff went down 25-21 in the final to John Spencer. Since

they were both friends of mine, I didn't really mind one way or the other. It was the first time a world champion had used a two-piece cue. John went on to beat me in the semi-final of the Canadian Open that year, which was played in a circus tent. He had scored a 146 in an earlier round. But he went down in the final to Higgins, who had come storming back into form after being excluded from 'Pot Black' that year.

My fellow-countryman Patsy Fagan suddenly burst into prominence by taking two tournaments on the trot – the UK title at Blackpool's Tower Circus and a one-day event at Wembley. Patsy later suffered from the 'yips', being psychologically unable to use the rest, and only recovered from his disability in the 1985 World Championship, when he put out Willie Thorne.

My successes have always tended to go in odd rather than even years, so I didn't do at all well in 1978. I went out in the first round of both the world championship (to Fred Davis) and the UK tournament, now sponsored by Coral at the Guildhall, Preston (to Doug Mountjoy, who went on to win it).

The feature of that season was Fred Davis's great comeback after a heart attack at the age of sixty-four. The BBC played the Beatles song 'When I'm 64' everytime he appeared on screen. Astonishingly, he reached the semi-final, losing a gripping match to Perrie Mans. Sadly, the tension of that match proved too much for his brother, the legendary Joe, who succumbed to a heart attack himself in the Crucible and died a few months afterwards. Two years later, Fred went on to win the world billiards title from Rex Williams, who had held it since 1968.

But I did register one success in 1978, when I broke the all-Irish record for a snooker break with 144 in an exhibition at St Comgall's Club, Larne. I remember I had a terrible cold and the organisers were pleased that I even bothered to turn up. They were less pleased when they saw how I was playing. In those clubs no drink is served in the snooker room, so many spectators stay in the bar and follow the play on a monitor screen while sipping a pint.

After the interval most of them stayed there and only a handful – presumably all teetotallers – wandered in to watch. I was playing Kevin Hughes, the snooker writer. After he had broken off I suddenly cleared the table and the crowds came rushing upstairs from the bar. You can never tell when these things are going to happen. I have a feeling that my first 147 break can't be too far away now.

John Spencer actually made the first 147 at a televised event at the Holsten Lager International at the Fulcrum Centre, Slough, in 1979. But there was a row with the technicians' union over the number of hours the crew were working – and the vital frame wasn't recorded. To add insult to injury, this was one of the few events that didn't offer a jackpot for maximum break! It was made even worse for John when he found himself on the receiving end of the first 147 actually shown on television – by Steve Davis in 1981. Barry Hearn, Steve's manager, must have made sure the cameras were turning that time.

Since 1979 was an odd year, I naturally did rather better. I was runner-up to Spencer in the Bombay Open and a semi-finalist in the Coral UK (losing to John Virgo, who went on to win his first major title). An oddity of the UK final was that Virgo won 14-13 after being forced to concede two frames to Terry Griffiths for arriving late at the final session. John, who looks such a mournful bearded figure on the screen, is actually the best mimic in the game, taking off my glasses to perfection in a very amusing routine.

I had already beaten Virgo in the semi-final of the World Championship, and earlier I had played some of my best snooker to eliminate Steve Davis and Ray Reardon. It was Steve's first taste of the Crucible atmosphere and he describes the match vividly in his book. It is worth repeating in view of what was to transpire between us six years later in the final. In some ways it reads almost like a dress-rehearsal:

As Dennis Taylor is probably the most humorous of all the snooker players, a lot of leg-pulling was guaranteed before we faced each other in the first round. Dennis wasted no time in launching into the wisecracks. When I asked him if Patricia planned to come up for the game, he simply said: 'No, not this one. She's just coming up for the final.'

You can never be offended by anything Dennis says. He loves to wind people up. And he is an expert at exchanging banter with hecklers in the crowd. His wit and skill make him very popular at the clubs, where he is in constant demand for exhibition matches between tournament appearances. Dennis is never nasty, never malicious, and he is a great sport.

Our match was tight from the start. I opened up with a 57, though the balls were so well placed I should have made a hundred. I lost position slightly and was forced to play from near the cushion and missed. To my horror, Dennis stepped in and mopped up with a 61.

Every single point was hard-earned by both of us. We ground on from 2-2 to 7-7 before Dennis pulled away to 9-7 and eventually to 12-9, needing just one more frame for the match.

At this point Dennis might have thought he had done enough to win, but I pulled myself together and managed to close the gap to 12-11. Dennis had suddenly lost his rhythm and, with the reds wide open, all I needed was a long blue into the top corner pocket to put me among them.

Call it pressure, call it inexperience – but I missed it. From that moment, Dennis regained control and won the match 13-11.

I couldn't help reflecting, when I read this account recently, that it was another miss on the blue in the deciding frame of our epic final that was to deprive Steve of his best chance of the match. Had he, too, remembered that earlier miss, if only for an instant? Memory plays strange tricks on the mind in snooker, never more than at moments of supreme pressure. Clive Everton says snooker players grow scar tissue in the mind like boxers do on their eyebrows.

I had played so well to defeat Reardon 13-8 in our quarter final in 1979 that I had become the favourite for the title, especially with Spencer, Thorburn and Higgins already out. It was certainly my best chance yet. I remember my parents and sisters came over from Ireland to see it. I was just thirty and recalled that people like Jack Rea had forecast that I would be world champion by then. All the portents seemed right.

Even my opponent didn't look too forbidding. Terry Griffiths was new. It was his first attempt at the title. On form I should have won, though Terry had beaten Higgins with a century break in the decider after one of the best matches anyone had ever seen. He had also come through a gruelling semi-final with Eddie Charlton, one session of which had gone on for five and a half hours. 'Steady Eddie' plays snooker with an in-built metronome like painting by numbers, but Terry didn't allow this to put him off. He takes his own time, anyway. For all his comparative inexperience, Terry had held himself together to win with a 97 clearance.

Terry had become an overnight TV superstar, a youthful flop-haired David against the ageing Goliaths of the green baize. The BBC were giving Wimbledon-style coverage to the event and the arrival of a new star was just what they wanted. I was the favourite, the man to beat, an unaccustomed role for me. I would have much preferred to be the underdog – the role I eventually played against Steve Davis six years later.

The match went wrong for me at the end of the second to last night. I was ahead by 15 frames to 13 with two to play. I had chances in both and should have gone into the final day with a four-frame lead. That would have been it. Had I opened up a gap like that at such a stage, I would have won. There were two crucial pressure shots that I should have got. Terry was able to inch his way back level at 15-all. I felt I'd blown it, which was no way to approach the final day.

Mind you, I was having terrible trouble with my contact lenses, which I was trying out for the first time in a major tournament. One of them was so sore I had to take it out. They were burning my eyes under the lights by the end of the evening. At the same time, they had dramatically improved my sight. I particularly remember noticing the metal ferrule shining on the end of the rest – I'd never seen it before.

Anyway, I collapsed on the final day – there's no other word for it – losing nine of the ten frames played. It was a nightmare. Clive Everton detected a nervous snatch at the back of my cueing action, which I fatally tried to correct by gripping the cue harder. Terry's grip is one of the loosest in the game.

Even though I had gone further than ever before and come second in the world, people thereafter began to characterise me as the eternal runner-up, as a player who lacked 'bottle' when the chips were down. The trouble with that kind of comment is that it gradually saps your confidence. You begin to half believe it yourself, no matter how hard you tell yourself it isn't true.

Janice Hale, a very nice lady who keeps the Press room on its toes, referred to me in the *Observer* as 'one of the circuit's supporting cast, a regular earner rather than a winner.'

I couldn't help recalling something that my old hero Jack Rea had once said about me: 'Dennis plays very well and he has a great chance of becoming one of the top professionals. But he will have to overcome an inferiority complex when he's playing the top men. When he knows he has the beating of someone he really goes to town, but when he is up against it he goes completely into a shell.' Is this what had happened here? I asked myself some hard questions in the following weeks – but I didn't find any easy answers.

I may have lost a World Championship, but I had gained a friend. Terry and I struck up an immediate friendship that has lasted ever since. We have even been on holiday together to Disneyland with our respective families.

I'll never forget that night of the 1979 world final – and not just because I won £5,000, my biggest prize so far. As I was pulling myself together in my dressing-room, there was a knock at the door. It was Terry. Would I give him and his wife, Annette, a lift to the celebration dinner? Oh – and another thing – would I mind taking the trophy there in the boot of my car?

I didn't know whether to laugh or to cry. Being me, of course, I couldn't help seeing the funny side of it.

PART FOUR

Have Cue, Will Travel (1980-84)

The 1980s opened for me on a high: I was ranked number two in the world. I was soon on another high – winging my way to India for the Bombay Open. When the Sixties dawned, my horizons had been limited to Coalisland and the surrounding fields of East Tyrone. The start of the Seventies had found me among Lancashire's satanic mills. Since then snooker had been my passport to a wider world, to Canada, Australia and the Far East. Now I was heading for the place where it all began.

Steve Davis and I played at the Bombay Gymkhana Club on a worn old table that carried echoes of the imperial past. That grand old Victorian character John Roberts, the W.G. Grace of the green baize, had come out to India a hundred years before us in the days of the Raj and carried billiard tables on the backs of elephants to the Maharajah of Jaipur. They all had billiard tables in their palaces in those days.

I actually met the Maharani of Jaipur at a dinner party out there. She was a marvellous lady. Like the other princely families of India, the Jaipurs had lost their traditional authority when the country gained independence from British rule in 1947. But the Maharani was a politician and was seeking election to the Indian Parliament as an MP.

I had a dance with her and told her all my Irish jokes, adapting them to the Sikhs. She thought they were hilarious and said she could use me in her election campaign if I'd go round the country telling them!

We had good crowds for the snooker in India and some splendid hospitality. I remember being invited to dinner by two brothers, who sent a car for us. We had no idea what to expect. We arrived at what looked like a twelve-storey block of flats, but it turned out to be their home – with a swimming pool on the top and four floors crammed with ancient Chinese jade. There were two whole floors of antique clocks. Just one piece of jade in one cabinet was worth about 20,000 dollars, so the whole collection must have been priceless.

We found that a bit hard to take, with people outside lying in the gutters. I found the pressure of people claustrophobic. Steve and I went out for a walk one night to get a bit of fresh air and I showed him the Gateway to India. Within five minutes we were surrounded by about forty kids wanting *baksheesh*.

Graham Miles and I were allocated a driver who looked after us and took us everywhere we wanted to go. His name was Gulan. He was a very nice modest lad and we tried to find out what he normally did for a living. Eventually he told us he was a scrap dealer, so we assumed he must walk around the streets of Bombay picking up scrap metal on a handcart or something. Later we discovered that he actually broke up ships for scrap and must have been very rich indeed!

The snooker boom is spreading to the East, with record sales of tables and TV programmes to places like Singapore, Malaysia, Thailand and Hong Kong. I like to think that our visits have helped to increase local interest in the game. Steve Davis and I have broken new ground by playing in Communist China, which is like potting the red and the yellow balls at the same time!

There are some very promising players over there: Gary Kwok, the Asian champion, in Hong Kong; Sakchai Sim-Ngarm and the fifteen-year-old Wattanu Pu-Oborn in Thailand; Lim Koon Guan in Singapore; two Indians, O.B. Agrawal, the world amateur snooker champion and Geet Sethi, the youngest-ever world amateur billiards champion, and (nearer home) the exciting young Maltese player, Tony Drago.

Already there are twenty-two nationalities represented at the world amateur championship, including unlikely countries such as Iceland, Sweden and Mauritius. I look forward to the day when they are all represented at the Crucible for the world professional tournament. We can then perhaps claim Olympic status!

Barry Hearn is trying to extend the boundaries even wider to include South America. He and Steve recently played in São Paulo, where Steve beat the Brazilian champion in front of forty million television viewers – twice as many as watched our final at the Crucible. The Brazilian champion calls himself Rui Chapeau and has said he'll never take his white hat off until he is beaten. Even when Steve beat him he wouldn't take it off, but presented Barry and Steve with white hats of their own instead.

In Singapore once we played snooker in a cricket club. We also went to the famous Change Alley, with its little stalls where they can sell you anything from a charm bracelet to a motor car. They were offering to make a lightweight suit in twenty-four hours, so we went for a fitting. I was changing behind a curtain and had just got down to my underpants when I saw the biggest rat I've ever seen in my life running across a beam. Meanwhile, our promoter, Maurice Hayes, had decided to play a practical joke, so he borrowed a feather duster from the girl assistant and shoved it under the curtain. I was just scrambling back into my trousers in a panic when I felt this tickling down my legs and assumed it must be the rat. I've never been so frightened in my life.

Graham Miles had a suit made there of a very expensive material because they'd told him it would resist cigarette burns. When he got to Australia he was telling everybody about this and saying how terrific it was that it wouldn't burn. So he shoved his cigarette against it to prove the point and burnt a great hole through the cloth!

On that trip to Australia Eddie Charlton was always grumbling about the English climate, saying he'd been going there for thirteen years and had never seen a patch of blue sky. I remember getting fed up with him about this as we sat freezing in the Australian basketball stadiums where we were playing in the evenings.

We had been presented with packs of Barossa wine everywhere we went, so when we had a weekend off I went to stay in a little motel in the Barossa Valley to see how the wine was made. It was only a little place and nobody else seemed to be staying there. There was absolutely nothing to do, so I went down from my room to see if I could borrow a bottle-opener for one of these presentation packs.

The owner of the motel was in the bar and seemed a bit lonely, so we started chatting away and he asked me where I came from. He invited me to have a drink and said he'd got a bottle of Jameson Whisky. So he went to the shelf and took the bottle down and blew the dust off and put two glasses on the counter and poured us a drink. I felt I was in a cowboy saloon. We finished up playing darts – he clearly hadn't talked to anybody for ages.

Eventually his daughter and her husband turned up with Eddie Charlton's brother, Jimmy, and after a few drinks they invited us to go out with them into the bush. This sounded like a great idea, especially after a few more drinks.

They loaned me a great big pair of filthy overalls, which had pockets full of bullets, I remember. We had a car and a Land Cruiser, so we put a big metal bath in the back containing about 120 bottles of beer in a pack of ice, and set off. The Land Cruiser had a big searchlight on the front for tracking kangaroos – that's what the bullets were for. They shoot them like pests around there.

We finally came to a halt after about three hours' driving and realised we were lost in the bush. We were only about sixty miles from Adelaide, but it was silent and dark and very creepy. We found some old ruins and Aborigine graves.

Then it started to pour with rain. Jimmy Charlton sat by the camp fire like an Indian chief with a shawl around his shoulders, drinking cans of beer on his own. Eddie Charlton says his brother is the only man in the world who trains to drink. He runs about ten miles a day to keep himself fit so that he can drink in the evening.

I wondered what I'd let myself in for. I wasn't going to sit in the rain and I wasn't going to sleep in those old ruins or among the graves. So I made a beeline for the car and curled up in the back. It rained all night and the car was stuck in a swamp. Fortunately, the Land Cruiser managed to beat a path through to the motel and I just managed to get to my exhibition in time to play Eddie Charlton. None of the spectators could have guessed what I'd just been through.

I remember in Canada once I was due to set off from the airport with Del Simmons, Ray Reardon and John Spencer. Ray wanted to get on the plane, but John said: 'No, let's wait until everybody's on and have a drink.' When we finally tried to board, Ray wasn't best pleased to discover that the plane had been overbooked and we couldn't get on. So we were sent back to town to a hotel.

We sat gloomily in the bar, fed up at the delay, then finally went to our rooms. I was surprised to find the light on in the room allocated to me, so I entered gingerly and was even more surprised to see an open bottle of champagne in an ice bucket, still half-full. Then I looked about me and saw a bottle of tablets open and some dirty magazines spread around the room. This is a bit funny, I thought.

I strode on warily into the bathroom and saw that the shower curtain was closed. My imagination raced in overtime: champagne, tablets, closed shower curtain – somebody had clearly done themselves in.

I knocked on Del's room and John's in a bit of a panic. I told them what I'd found and they hurried along to the room with me – Del, the hard man, at the front, John bringing up the rear. We crept silently into the bathroom, our pulses racing. Del was just about to pull back the shower curtain when a terrible bloodcurdling scream rang out. Del and I leapt in the air in terror, and it took us several seconds to realise that it was just one of Spencer's practical jokes.

There was nothing behind the curtain when we finally plucked up the courage to look. All that had happened was that an airline pilot had suddenly been called on duty and had left in a hurry, leaving things lying around.

Travelling on the snooker circuit produces dozens of funny stories. I remember once playing with Willie Thorne at Leatherhead at a show fixed up by Colin Reid, who arranged snooker evenings for a number of players. Willie and I were sharing a room in Colin's house. After the show we were separated and Willie stayed on with some friends he had met. I left at about 1 a.m. and went to bed.

Willie turned up about 3.30 in the morning and found the door locked. There was an Alsatian at the back and children in bed, so he didn't like to make too much noise hammering on the door. He tried shouting up at the window without success, then started lobbing up all the coins in his pocket to attract my attention. But there was six inches of snow on the ground and the coins disappeared when they fell to earth. He couldn't catch them in the dark.

When he'd got through the ten pences in his pocket, he tried another ploy. He found a bicycle in the garage and a brush. He leaned the bicycle against the wall and stood on it, then tapped the upstairs window with a brush. I heard the tap on the window and thought to myself: who can be tapping on an upstairs window? It must be a giant out there. I didn't fancy opening the window because I didn't know what I'd find.

Then I realised it was Willie's voice whispering 'Dennis, Dennis!', so I went downstairs and round the back to see what was going on. When I got there he was still standing on the bicycle shouting 'Dennis, Dennis!' while I was peering after him in the dark, whispering 'Willie, Willie!' When we finally got into the bedroom we rolled around for fully three-quarters of an hour. We roared with laughter just thinking about the whole thing.

Willie is another of my pals on the circuit, a great character. He runs a club in Leicester and has a whole cast of supporters who follow him everywhere, mostly gamblers like himself. They sound like characters from 'Guys and Dolls': Racing Raymond, Creamcake and Billy the Dip.

I've always believed as a philosophy of life that if you can't say something good about someone, then don't say anything. There is nobody on the circuit I haven't been able to get on with, including Alex Higgins, though he can sometimes be more of a trial than most. I've always admired Alex as a player and he has done a lot for the game of snooker. I never disagree with him for the sake of disagreeing and I never agree with him for the sake of agreeing. I just state my mind and I'd like to think he has quite a bit of respect for me. I can tell two stories that show the different sides of his character.

I was once booked for five nights of exhibitions with Alex in the Exeter area. I checked in to a nineteen-bedroom hotel, thinking I'd have a quiet time, then found Alex was staying there too. It was so quiet they weren't used to people staying up late. But the night porter turned out to be a snooker fan who worshipped Alex, so he'd do anything for us. Alex used to go into the kitchen with him and make enormous cheese sandwiches. When he came out it was like a pound of cheese on each slice of bread.

Alex got this fellow so confused he could make him believe anything. He told him that he could hypnotise anyone by making them stare at the medallion round his neck. The poor chap didn't dare look at Alex after that. One night Alex invited one of the waitresses for a drink. She was Spanish but spoke perfect English, and the porter didn't know her nationality. When the man was out making the cheese sandwiches Alex told the girl he was going to pretend to hypnotise her.

When the porter came back he found Alex waving the medallion in front of the girl and saying she must go to sleep. Then Alex said: 'I'm going to count to three and when I snap my fingers you are to wake up and speak in Spanish.' He counted to three, snapped his fingers, and the girl started babbling in fluent Spanish.

The porter's eyes were popping out of his head. Alex turned to him and said: 'Now, would you like to speak Chinese?' The man fled.

By this time he believed everything Alex told him, so Alex took full advantage to keep us all amused. He told him he was a stunt man and had gone over Niagara Falls in a barrel. The man swallowed this as well.

Alex made a massive order for drinks for a fictional party, and when the man said he was afraid the noise might disturb the other guests, Alex put on a serious look.

'Don't worry,' he said, 'I have this friend with an electrical shop. He'll put these synthesisers on each wall and one on the ceiling to block out the noise and you won't hear the music anywhere.' The man looked suitably reassured and we just stopped ourselves bursting out laughing. It went on like this every night.

There is, of course, another side to Alex: what one might call the McEnroe syndrome. I was on the receiving end of it in the final of the Tolly Cobbold Classic at Ipswich in 1980. I was leading 3-1 at the time and laid a snooker. Alex had to swerve the cue-ball to get out of it and hit the red and black balls simultaneously. This is known as a split ball and is a foul. The referee called it: seven points away. It had nothing to do with me; I wasn't even near.

Alex simply wouldn't accept the decision and argued interminably that he had hit the red ball first. There was no way it could possibly be proved either way. As far as I'm concerned, that's what referees are there for – to make those awkward hairline decisions. It wasn't up to me to overrule the referee just because Alex was upset about it. The referee was in a position to see and I wasn't. Furthermore, he wasn't an interested party.

Eventually Alex had to stop arguing and get on with the game. Then the trouble really started, because the referee gave me a free ball since I hadn't a clear sight of the red after Alex's foul shot. This time Alex went berserk. He simply wouldn't have it. He got up off his chair and invited people from the crowd to judge whether it should be a free ball or not. You simply can't do that. I just stayed away from the whole thing and sat down in my chair. I have never had a go at Alex, no matter how hard he has tried to provoke me. Meanwhile, the cameras on Anglia Television were soaking up the whole incident, as Alex doubtless knew.

Then, a few minutes later, as he was walking around

the table to take a shot, he muttered audibly: 'Bloody cheat!' That was me gone. I couldn't hit a ball after that. I lost the match 5-4.

There are some people who thrive on arguments and the tensions they stir up. It seems to turn them on and release hidden energies. I'm not one of them. Even as a child, I couldn't bear any aggro. Alex loves it – and for the same reason as McEnroe does: it's a useful psychological weapon in his armoury when the balls are running against him. It's like a chess player who tips over the board when he's losing. Because it's going wrong on the table you lunge at the man instead.

I would have been happy to let this incident rest in peace if Alex hadn't raised it in his *Snooker Scrapbook* in a way that was plainly directed at me. 'Opponents who are willing to stand by and see me fouled by the referee unfairly and yet say nothing', he wrote, 'must be pretty desperate to beat me by any means they can.' He cites Anglia TV's action replay in support of his case that he didn't foul the black, but it didn't prove anything at all.

It struck me as peculiarly ironic, in the light of all that fuss, to see Alex sit silent in his chair in the semi-final of the UK Coral tournament in 1984 when Cliff Thorburn was penalised by the referee for failing to nominate a ball. Practically everyone else in the country had seen him name the green on TV. I don't know what I would have done myself in that situation. Had I actually heard Cliff nominate the colour, I would have felt obliged to speak up. Otherwise I would have had to leave it to the referee. I'm not saying Alex was wrong to keep silent, because he may not have heard. But in leaving it to the referee he was doing exactly the same thing that he accused me of doing. He can't have it both ways.

But then Alex does want it both ways – in fact, he wants it all ways. And good luck to him, in a sense, if he wants to win so badly. But there's surely enough genuine tension in the game already without these theatrical displays of frustration. If I'm beaten because I can't cope with the pressure generated by the skill of my opponent's play, that's one thing. But to be beaten because my opponent cannot control his childish bad temper is something else. Professional players are entitled to some protection against that.

I'm the last person to want all personality eliminated from the snooker table. A contest between faceless, unsmiling automatons would be very boring – you might as well let the two cues sort it out between them or have a computer decide the result. They are actually trying to build a snooker-playing robot at Bristol University. I'm all for humanising the game – and that's clearly what the public also like about it. But it is essentially a game of skill and concentration and it can only be practised at the highest level under the right conditions.

You wouldn't expect a world-class pianist to play at his best if the audience were crunching crisps very loudly, any more than you'd expect Sandy Lyle to sink a putt if his opponent was waving a club at him on the green or muttering under his breath.

Alex Higgins is such a mass of contradictions that – deep down inside him – I think he knows this too. If not, why should he have thrust £100 on my friend Terry Griffiths after the Ipswich affair and asked him to give it to me? Needless to say, I told him where to put it.

But on reflection I can see that this readiness to apologise, even when it's too late or not enough, is one of Alex's redeeming features, a sign that he is still trying – with difficulty and often without much success – to save himself from a self-destructive urge within his own nature. I sincerely hope he succeeds – for all our sakes, especially his own.

Alex's worst fault, in my view, is not the way he treats other players, but the way he treats his fans. Players can usually look after themselves – and if they can't, there's a professional body to help them – but the fans are often wide-eyed and vulnerable young kids. I've seen Alex abuse them and even threaten them with physical violence – just because they've asked for his autograph at a moment he found inconvenient.

These are the people who, in the end, are paying for his food and drink. The time to worry about autograph hunters is when they stop. Alex gets more fan mail than any other player, but I doubt if he answers it all, or even most of it. He has been known to throw some of it away unopened.

Trish and I sit down at the dining table and deal with mine. It's sometimes a chore, especially when you're tired, but it has to be done. After all, it's a human contact you've made with someone, a living relationship – you can't just deny it like that.

I've always found that the best answer to Alex is on the snooker table, and I'm glad to say that I achieved this in 1980, the same year as the row at Tolly Cobbold, by taking the Irish championship from him in the Ulster Hall, Belfast, by 21 frames to 15. He admitted afterwards that this made him 'sick to the stomach'. I felt correspondingly elated at finally winning what I still regarded as my national crown.

It had always eluded me until then. Having got my hands on it at last, I wasn't about to give it up easily and held it for three years in succession. Had it been a Lonsdale belt for boxing, I could have kept it. I'm proud to say that I still hold it today.

Higgins won three other tournaments that year and was runner-up in four more – most dramatically in the final of the World Championship to Thorburn. The snooker was interrupted – much to the annoyance of fans – by live coverage of the SAS raid that ended the Iranian embassy siege in London.

I had to content myself with winning the Open final at Pontin's Festival of Snooker, being runner-up to Steve Davis in the Wilsons Classic, and reaching the semi-final in a new event, the British Gold Cup.

But I did lose one crown that I greatly prized – the pro-celebrity snooker on TV, which comedian Bill Maynard and I won three times. I smartened up my comedy act through mixing with these funny characters and learned a great deal from them about the importance of timing.

Once we were playing against David Taylor, the 'Silver Fox', who advised his partner to play a semi-stun shot. 'What's a semi-stun shot?' said his partner. Before David could reply, Bill Maynard chipped in: 'Quite simple, really. If you miss the red, he'll hit you over the head with the cue!'

Les Dawson was the supreme master of timing. In one game I was partnered by Kenny Lynch, who was about to pot a black on the edge of the pocket. Just as he brought the cue back Les said, very quietly: 'I wouldn't pot that if I were you, Kenny. It might be a relative.'

He also did his best to upstage me when I was about to make a century break on the programme. Just as I lined up the crucial shot in total silence he exclaimed: 'Your flies are open!' The audience roared with laughter and I collapsed on the table. Not to be outdone, I backed off the set, pretending to hold my trousers together, then reappeared in a new pair. This time I made the pot and went on to make 125 amid tremendous applause.

Another thing the pro-celebrity snooker taught me was how to ignore distractions and not let them affect my concentration. Mind you, I guess I'd learned that early on at Gervin's already, for there was always plenty going on around the table there. I remember once playing an exhibition at Hillsborough when a drunken man was dragged out and bumped down every stair while

I was playing. I suppose that all stood me in good stead.

But it's something else to avoid distractions when you're under the television lights and know that your every move or facial expression is going to be seen by millions of people – and that a remark, once made, can't be taken back.

Snooker players always seem to have got on well with showbiz folk. We're all entertainers, I suppose – and we're all nightbirds. Joe Davis even appeared on stage at the London Palladium during the war – playing trick shots that were magnified to the audience by means of a huge angled mirror. Joe also married a showgirl, June Malo, while she was playing Dandini in pantomime.

What I like about meeting showbiz people is not only their company, which is always good fun, but that it gives me a chance to introduce them to my family. Dad was thrilled to meet Jimmy Tarbuck, for example. When he's back home in his little house watching Jimmy Tarbuck on television, it must give him a nice warm feeling to think that he's met him. After a while I've come to take that sort of thing for granted, but it's nice for the folks. It means they get something extra out of my success and I like that.

I was picking up hints all the time to improve my exhibition routine. My mentor in my early days was Jack Rea, who was the funniest player on the circuit for many years. He had a great routine of trick shots, including rolling the balls up and down parallel cues. He didn't tell jokes as such but he chatted away to the audience in an engaging fashion. It was his personality as much as anything he said. Ray Reardon was also the master of trick shots and light repartee.

But I had noticed that, even with the best routines, there was an awkward silence as they set up their trick shots. I decided to fill this with my Irish jokes, which were also handy when the tricks failed first time, as they are often inclined to do. I remember thinking to myself: why not smooth over the awkward pauses with some jokes?

I've always found when I'm playing, even in major tournaments, that little jokes and funny remarks come naturally to me. Perhaps they are a form of nervous release. You should really be concentrating on your snooker all the time, of course, but it is difficult to let an incident go by when you want to make a quip. I find it hard to resist the temptation. I try to hold the jokes back when there are two tables in use, in case the audience laughs and this upsets the other players. I also have to be careful who I'm playing against, since some people don't like it.

One of my problems these days is finding new jokes because other players keep pinching them. Terry Griffiths started telling Irish jokes when we became pals after the 1979 final. The worst culprit is my friend Willie Thorne, who has taken over pretty well my whole routine, having seen me do it every night for three weeks in South Africa. It can be embarrassing if I go to a club and tell a joke and they say: 'We heard that one two weeks ago – Willie Thorne was here.' I have to check these days that he hasn't been to a club ahead of me.

When I think how shy I used to be as a boy, I can hardly believe it when I see myself on television cracking jokes to millions of people or chatting merrily to Terry Wogan or Russell Harty. But I was brought up in a hard school in Lancashire snooker – that's the part of the world known as the comedians' graveyard. I had to learn to look after myself.

I remember once a truculent voice in a crowd shouting, 'Can you get it in?' as I lined up a shot. 'Well, I could if the pockets were as big as your mouth,' I replied – and immediately I could sense that the crowd were on my side. Humour can be a powerful weapon with people. It can also be a useful self-defence.

When Steve Davis whitewashed me 9-0 in the final of the Jameson International in 1981, the match was over so early that the crowd needed entertaining to get their money's worth. So I had to go straight back to the scene of my humiliation and make people laugh, no matter how I might be feeling inside.

Jean Rafferty, a writer who followed the circuit that year, reported in her book, *The Cruel Game*:

> It's an inhuman request to make of any sportsman, but his performance is as brave and gracious as any champion's display on the table. For forty minutes he makes people laugh, entertains them with trick shots and eases the awkwardness of the situation with his dry self-deprecating wit.
>
> Steve Davis sits slouched in his chair cold-faced. There is not a flicker of expression on his face as the affable Irishman redeems the humiliation of defeat and turns the evening into a triumph of character.
>
> Davis's head is bent. He has had the most complete victory any sportsman could wish for. He has crushed his opponent completely and yet it is the other man the people will be talking about as they go home, his jokes they will be laughing about.

At the time I didn't see it like that. I just felt I had to entertain people because I'd let them down. I was a bit like a plaintive puppy wagging its tail after being kicked. I was also clowning to stop myself crying. I realise now, after all that has happened since – especially against Steve – that evenings like that may have served a deeper purpose that only emerged under the severest pressure in the Crucible.

Deep down Steve knew my character couldn't be beaten and submerged, no matter how well he played or how often he came out ahead on the scoreboard. There's a part of me that never admits defeat. He knew I'd have something to spare, enough to make a joke when he was all coiled up inside, and – who knows? – perhaps that knowledge was just enough to haunt him when it really mattered.

If that sounds a shade fanciful, don't forget that snooker is as much about character as technique. To win you have to perform under the pressure of a big event all the shots that others can only do on the practice table. When it comes to pure technique, there is little to choose among the top dozen players, perhaps even the top twenty or thirty. We can all make the cue-ball do virtually anything except talk – when it doesn't really matter, that is.

Conversely, under the cosh – and especially under the television lights – I've seen big men tremble over shots they could do blindfolded ninety-nine times out of a hundred. Even me. I'm talking about the past, of course: it couldn't happen to me now. Not until the next time anyway!

Joe Davis used to say: 'It's the easy ones that are difficult.' I know what he meant. When I was 7-5 down in the world semi-final to Steve Davis in 1984, I was 64 points up with a possible 65 on the table. I cracked open the reds and was all set for a big break. I'd done the difficult bit. Then I hit a simple red too thin to the centre pocket, and it was all over. I was 9-5 down and going blurry at the edges before I could pull myself together – and by then it was too late.

Mine was just a miss under pressure. For a vital moment I had melted in the heat of the Crucible. But the experience strengthened me: I was tempered for the fire next time. In the case of older players, however, the tell-tale sign of decline is missing a simple shot when you're under no pressure at all.

It's a curious thing about snooker that you reach your fullest knowledge of the game just when your body is ceasing to do all that you ask of it. You know exactly what to do, but the hand or eye won't obey.

It's the same in golf. Arnold Palmer didn't stop being number one because he could no longer hit massive drives or iron shots – but because he began to miss the short putts. I've seen the same thing happen in snooker – to John Spencer and Ray Reardon, the giants of the game when I first turned pro. In both cases it was a matter of eyesight.

John has an ocular condition that means he has to take steroids all the time to control his eyelids and prevent double vision. Ray stubbornly refuses to wear glasses – he has tried out green eye-shields instead at a couple of tournaments. If he has never been used to wearing glasses, I can understand how awkward he must feel in them.

This is one subject on which I can reasonably claim to know what I'm talking about. As a kid I used glasses at school – I needed them to see the blackboard, even from the front row. But I couldn't wear them outside the classroom – vanity, I suppose. And I learned to play snooker without them.

At school I had a little pair of National Health Service specs with one of the sides missing. I would never wear them anyway, so they were just slung on the desk. I did all my work off the blackboard holding one side up while the other lens kept dropping out, so I'd be holding one side up to put the lens back in.

Since I'd always played snooker without the glasses, I never knew any difference. I thought the balls were always that size! When I began to wear contact lenses in about 1979 I saw the balls much bigger than before – and, of course, the pockets. I'd been playing the game in proportion, so to speak, but in miniature.

Snooker is a funny game visually. You have to look at two balls – the cue-ball and the target-ball – and at the pocket, almost simultaneously. It's not so much a question of eyesight as of eye-hand co-ordination. In cricket you need the same co-ordination, but there's only one ball and it's moving.

The key to snooker is the straightness of your cueing action. Even if your sight is weaker than somebody else's when measured by an optician, it doesn't matter too much if you can hit exactly what you are aiming to hit.

In snooker the double focus can make your eyes blur as you get older. But I've managed to reverse the process. I am actually seeing the balls better at the age of thirty-six than I did when I was twelve, or even nine when I first started playing. Steve Davis was good enough to say in Sheffield that I was the only one of the older players whose game had actually improved since he first came to the top five or six years ago. The reason is simple: I can see so much better.

I had terrible trouble with the contact lenses. They were so painful I couldn't keep them in. I realise now that that was probably to do with my reddish skin complexion, which is very sensitive. It can't stand much sun, for example. The eyeballs were probably irritated and inflamed by the foreign body, just as my skin is influenced by the sun.

I've had the most painful and humiliating experiences as a result of sun-tan. I remember lying once in agony in a cold bath for three hours in the Oberoi-Sheraton Hotel in Bombay and thinking I was going to die and nobody would ever know. I'd heard that yoghurt was good for inflamed skin, so I sent out for some. They could only get the fruity sort, which doesn't have the same properties as natural yoghurt, but I was so desperate that I smeared myself with it anyway. It dried in patchy lumps with big bits of strawberry sticking out. I was so unsightly that I even scared myself when I looked in the mirror. It hurt even more when I laughed.

The contact lenses were so painful I went back to playing without them for a year. But I knew that I could see better in them, so it always niggled me to have a go with the glasses. But I thought the glasses wouldn't work because of the magnifying effect. I thought they might distort my vision somehow, especially when I bent down to the shot.

I consulted Jack Karneham, the snooker coach and commentator, because he had trained in the family business as an optician. He told me that if I got them designed correctly they would be OK. In the end, Jack designed them himself. He worked at them in his garage one weekend with his old optician's kit, filing away. It was marvellous to watch.

People who joke that I've got my glasses on upside down are really quite right, because Jack put the main part of the lens at the top rather than the bottom, so that they look as though they are sitting on my forehead. When I bend down over the table I find I'm looking through the right bit.

The effect on my play has been remarkable. A long pot to the top pocket off the blue spot is a totally different proposition for me now. It was seeing the metal glittering on the end of the rest that made me realise what I'd been missing all those years.

I suppose my preference for a left-handed shot, rather than using the rest, may have had something to do with my eyesight too. I instinctively shied away from the long reach for a shot if I could possibly avoid it. I learned to play with my left hand because kids often refused to play with me *unless* I went left-handed. So I became very good at it. Joe Davis had the same experience in Chesterfield, where miners would only bet against him at 'Pink Pool' if he played them left-handed.

Steve Davis dominated 1981 in the way nobody had done since Higgins burst on the scene in 1972. As Jean Rafferty wrote: 'One image is left of the season – Steve Davis holding up the winner's tropy, flashlights exploding all around him like champagne, gleaming silver cups flashing bright as fireworks under the television lights, Steve Davis winning and winning and winning.'

That was the year Steve whitewashed me 9-0 in the Jameson, having already beaten me in the final of the Wilsons Classic. He went on to win the Yamaha trophy, where he beat me in the semi-final, the Courage trophy, and then the biggest one of all, the World Championship. To get there he had to beat White, Higgins, Griffiths, Thorburn and Mountjoy, so nobody could possibly begrudge him the title.

I reached one final the next year, going down to Steve in the final of the Tolly Cobbold. But there was a shock in the World Championship when Davis, Griffiths and Thorburn all went out in the first round. That should have been my big chance, but I allowed Silvino Francisco, playing there for the first time, to beat me 10-7.

That turned out to be Higgins' comeback year when he had that famous tear-stained reunion before the TV cameras at the Crucible with his wife Lynn and baby Lauren. Nobody had given him a chance because he had been having his worst season, but Alex is never so dangerous as when he is feeling wounded or ignored. He's like a sleeping tiger in this respect.

It was good to see Alex at last getting a major share of the rewards he had helped to bring to the game. His prize of £25,000 was quite an improvement on the £480 he had won in 1972. 'They fine me more than that nowadays,' he had commented wryly. The contrast was even greater with the sum of six pounds ten shillings that Joe Davis received when he won the first World Championship in

1927 – and he had to spend half that to buy the trophy!

The fact that Alex was world champion made it all the more satisfying that I had beaten him in the Irish professional championship – a tournament that has always mattered to both of us more than we usually care to admit. That year was an especially good one to win because it was the first time it had been an open tournament, in which all eight Irish professionals could enter. It took place at the Riverside Theatre, Coleraine, and I beat Higgins 16-13 in the final, having once been 14-8 up.

Previously the Irish title had been settled on a challenge match basis. I remember being rather put out in 1978 when Alex accepted a challenge from Patsy Fagan rather than from me. I had wanted to redeem myself after a bad beating from Alex the year before. His argument, as I recall, was that he had to play Fagan because he was from the South and I was a fellow-Northerner.

When I became the holder myself, I bowed to the force of Alex's logic and accepted Fagan's challenge. But by then, of course, Alex had changed his tune and felt resentful that he couldn't have another crack at the title himself. An open event, which eliminated the need for this bickering, was obviously a more satisfactory solution from every point of view.

It's a good job I did hold on to the Irish championship because I wasn't winning anything else. I had a poor season going into 1983 and ran some risk of slipping out of the top sixteen placings. This is important because it means you automatically qualify for a number of tournaments. I had been number thirteen for two years and I was beginning to get superstitious.

In the 1983 Jameson I went out in the second round to Cliff Thorburn. There was much comment on our slow play and somebody suggested that Cliff's autobiography should be called *Around the Table in Eighty Days*. To add injury to insult, I was stung by a wasp on the golf course. A worse fate befell me on the same golf course when Des Heather, from Jameson's, decided we could each have one free throw. I played a shot close to the hole – and was astonished to see Des pick up my ball and hurl it in the hedge. 'That's my free throw,' he said.

Cliff and I were invited to judge a beauty contest in a night-club, and he then went on to the final, where he lost to Steve Davis. You always feel better about losing in an early round if the chap who beats you goes on to the final.

Young Mike Hallett from Grimsby put me out of the Lada Classic and Jimmy White saw me off in the Coral UK. The final of the Coral UK that year was one of the game's great classic recoveries. Alex Higgins came back from a 0-7 whitewash in the opening session to beat Steve Davis 16-15 in the final frame.

Steve never really recovered from that turn-around. As Clive Everton said, 'One of life's fundamental certainties was shaken in his mind.' He began to have a nagging doubt about his own capacity to hold a long lead under pressure. That doubt was still present in Steve's mind – or lurking in his subconscious – in the Crucible in April 1985. For I too was to come back from the dead against Steve – in my case from 0-8 behind.

Rex Williams and I were partnered in the Hofmeister world doubles. Rex is one of the big names in the game and an influential figure as chairman of the players' body, the World Professional Billiards and Snooker Association. He won the amateur snooker championship at the age of seventeen and turned professional in 1951. He challenged old Clark McConachy for the world billiards championship in 1968 and held the title until Fred Davis took it from him in 1980.

In 1952 Rex played against Alec Brown, the man who had become famous at Thurston's in 1938 for pulling out the 'fountain pen cue', just a few inches long, to move the cue-ball out of a pack of reds. The stroke was banned and a new rule introduced that a cue had to be at least three feet in length.

Rex challenged Pulman unsuccessfully for the world snooker title on two occasions and might well have won it if the professional game hadn't gone into decline while he was at his peak. He lost narrowly in the semi-final to Higgins in 1972 and would probably have won if he had potted a straight blue across the table. That was the Year of the Hurricane – so the whole history of the modern game might have been different if Rex had sunk that blue.

Rex also built up a successful business career making and leasing out tables to clubs. He is one of my partners in the ITV commentary box. As partners on the table we had less success, however, going out in the second round of the world doubles.

My fortunes picked up in the Benson and Hedges Irish Masters of 1984, where I reached the semi-final, losing to Griffiths, who in turn lost to Davis in the final. But I was still at risk of dropping out of the top sixteen unless I won my first round match at the Crucible in the World Championship.

As luck would have it, I was drawn against Joe Johnson, who had just knocked out Jimmy White and Cliff Thorburn in the Players' tournament and then lost the final to Tony Knowles by only one frame. He had also made a maximum break and was in cracking form. All the seeds were hoping to avoid him that year. Anyway, I trounced him 10-1, then beat Parrott and Mountjoy to reach the semi-final. Even though I lost there to Davis – after missing that crucial red to the centre pocket – it was enough to lift me to eleventh place in the rankings.

The biggest sensation at the Crucible that year was away from the snooker table. It was a torrid series on sex

111

in the *Sun* by Tony Knowles – 'Why They Call Me the Hottest Pot in Snooker'. He wrote about having three or more girls in bed and one was shown in nothing but her suspenders draped across the green baize. He claimed that one woman had flown him off by helicopter for a night of passion.

Like many of the players, I was sorry to see the game lowered to this X-certificate level. I supported the fine of £5,000 imposed on Tony by the WPBSA for bringing the game into disrepute, even if it only made a small dent in the sum he is said to have received from the paper. I was also sorry for Tony's parents, who can't have enjoyed seeing this sensational stuff. I'm sure Tony must now regret the whole business. It has certainly done his own or snooker's reputation no good at all.

He came to prominence with a splash when he beat Steve Davis 10-1 in the first round of the World Championship of 1982 and quickly rose to number two in the world rankings. But he has never quite lived up to his promise, perhaps because he allows himself to be too easily upset when things aren't going his way. On his day, though, he can be an aggressive potter and a hard man to beat – as I was soon to find out for myself.

The snooker season used to run parallel with the soccer season from September to May. When I started, the pros used to put their cues away for the summer, just getting them out for the occasional practice. Some players didn't even do that. But there are a number of summer events on the calendar now, including oveseas tours and holiday camp tournaments. But I still like to take a good break in the summer and Trish has always tried to arrange things so that we have a fair amount of time together as a family.

During the summer of 1984 Tony Knowles beat me in the first round of the Australian Winfield Masters, but as he went on to win the tournament I didn't feel I'd done so badly. And at least I didn't have to share a room this time with Eddie Charlton. Eddie is a keep-fit fanatic and had once dragged me into his routine, ordering a health-giving breakfast for me of fruit juice, yoghurt and milk while he did his exercises, then forcing me out on a six-mile run.

I did much better in Spain, winning the first Costa del Sol Classic in the ballroom of Las Palmeras Hotel, Fuengirola. We played to capacity houses, mainly British holidaymakers. This event may catch on if it gets more backing from the tour companies and may set a trend for more tournaments on the European mainland. Many of these countries are now getting our snooker programmes on TV, which should stimulate interest.

So I entered the 1984/85 season in good shape, with the glasses now feeling great and the threat of being relegated a thing of the past. I had played my way out of trouble. I was much happier with my cue, which was two inches longer and a fraction wider at the tip (10 millimetres) than I'd used in the past. Oddly enough, the cue had been lying around the house for twelve months before I thought to use it.

Steve Davis was again everybody's favourite for the new season, but I was glad to see that Alexander Clyde of the London *Standard* gave me an honourable mention in his preview: 'Call me naïve if you like, but I have one fervent wish as the young millionaires set off on another chase for that pot of gold – to see a few of the also-rans depositing some egg on those illustrious faces from time to time.' Among these 'also-rans' he included 'the hilarious Dennis Taylor, whose presence in the press room is like a breath of fresh air'.

He wrote that compliment in the programme for the snooker writers' dinner, the traditional start to the new season. It was taking place at the Redwood Lodge and Country Club, near Bristol, the scene of my first tournament victory as a professional. It was a very happy affair, giving the wives a chance to dress up and have a night out before taking up their accustomed role as snooker widows when the season proper got under way.

I was delighted when the journalists named me Snooker Personality of the Year. Willie Thorne and I, who seem to be regarded as the comedians of the circuit, were called upon to do our party pieces, and a good time was had by all. Somebody made the point at the dinner that there are few sports where the players, the press, the sponsors, the promoters and the governing body can all get together like this for such a friendly occasion.

The snooker writers are a motley crowd. They have always been good to me, so I mustn't complain. They have a difficult job to do and it can't be much fun sitting in airless press rooms for days or even weeks on end, especially when the play goes on so late into the night they miss their deadlines.

Some know their snooker better than others, but a few of them seem to have no interest at all in what goes on in the arena and are looking instead for scandalous stories about drugs or sex, or bribing players with money to say unfriendly things about each other.

I suppose it's the price of success, in that snooker players are now front-page news as well as back-page news. We have Higgins to thank for that, as for so much else. Having seen us on their television screens and got used to us like characters in a soap opera, people want to know all about our private lives as well. We're like figures in 'Dallas' or 'Coronation Street', somewhere between J.R. and Ken Barlow. (Come to think of it, Barry Hearn has a look of J.R.!)

My own private life isn't normally such as to excite the interest of the *News of the World*, so you can imagine my surprise – not to mention Trish's – when I was pictured there between a pair of pretty girls. What happened (this is my story and I'm sticking to it!) is that I'd been taken along to Stringfellows, the trendy London discotheque, after an exhibition. A photographer was lying in wait as soon as I got there, with a pop group, the Little Foxes. The bulb had popped and the picture was in the paper before I even knew who they were. I expect the photographer did very nicely out of it.

That was my first taste of the publicity machine, which seems to grind on saying what it wants to say regardless of the truth or the facts or anything as dull as that. I was not best pleased to open the parish magazine in Coalisland recently and see myself quoted as saying: 'This is the most successful time in my career. I have never been so rich or so happy and I've been treated like a lord. I go everywhere in a Cadillac which has a cocktail cabinet and a TV set in it. My world has changed completely – and I'm loving it.'

This had been picked up from a British newspaper. Anybody who knows me at all must realise that those are the kind of sentiments I'd never let past my lips even if I felt them – which I don't. When you're as quick on the draw as I am with words it's sometimes hard enough to live with what I *did* say, let alone what I didn't.

By this time, with the Costa del Sol Classic under my belt, I was eager to get cracking on the circuit proper. The first big money tournament of the season was the Jameson International. This took place at the Eldon Square Recreation Centre, Newcastle-upon-Tyne. The problem facing Willie Thorne and myself, however, was that we were somewhere else at the time – on the Shetland Islands, to be precise.

We had flown there on the Thursday for an exhibition after being assured that there would be no problem getting back by Sunday. We woke up Friday morning to find the island shrouded in mist. There was no question of a flight out because no planes had been able to fly in. But there were still two days before we had to be in Newcastle, so we stilled our rising panic, reached for a calming drink, and stayed over for another night.

Next morning was just the same. Willie started ringing round and found a private pilot ready to fly us to the mainland – at a price. The price was £750 – more than we'd got for the exhibition. We had ho option really. We had a table fitter with us who crouched in the back of the plane with his tool bag. It was a memorable flight to Aberdeen, but when we reached there on Saturday night we found there were no overnight trains to Newcastle.

In the end we persuaded a Scottish cabbie to drive us through the night at a cost of £150. I was able to curl up in the back for a sleep but poor Willie had to listen to the driver's Celtic chatter. Despite this, Willie went straight to the table next day and beat Dene O'Kane of New Zealand 5-3.

In fact, we both won our first two matches without any trouble. I was in the groove, cueing very well, and I was beginning to fancy my chances for the tournament. If I could beat Silvino Francisco, I'd be through to the semi-final. When I went into the TV commentary box on the Wednesday night to judge the shot of the tournament, I was feeling pretty good.

When I came out I was shattered. I received the news that my mother had suddenly died in Coalisland. It's hard to describe the shock this gave me. To understand that you'd need to know all that my mother meant to me, and that is something I can't bring myself to talk about even now. Nothing like this had ever happened to me in all my life. It was like a knife going in.

The next morning Trish and I went to Ireland for the funeral, along with my aunts from Blackburn and the rest of the family. My mother was the eldest of six sisters and their natural leader and confidante. We were all devastated.

There had been no warning. When she collapsed, my father called the doctor and my sister Jean came round. The doctor didn't think it was her heart, but went to get the cardiograph machine to check. While he was out she had a sudden massive heart attack in the armchair, and died. Jean was with her and said she suffered no pain.

The pain was ours. We all feel it still. It was not just her dying, but the shock of it. She had been so active, the life and soul of the party, the magnet for all of us. Everybody knew her in Coalisland, where she had lived and worked all her life, running the Evergreen Club for the pensioners. We had all taken shelter in her strong personality. Now that shelter was gone, and we were alone. The one small consolation was that she had lived long enough to enjoy her fortieth wedding anniversary, a happy occasion with all the family around her.

I took her death very badly. People said they could see it in me. I felt so helpless. I didn't know what to do. I thought I should stay on and help the family through it. But my father and Trish took me aside after the funeral and told me to go back to the snooker and get stuck in, so that I had something to do. 'Go back and win one for her,' they said. 'You know that's what she would want.'

I returned in time for the final phase of the Rothmans Grand Prix at the Hexagon, Reading, one of the best venues in snooker. I was still feeling dazed but I found that Dad and Trish were right: the snooker gave me something to concentrate on and stopped me brooding alone.

My first opponent was Reardon, never an easy man to beat, though he had recently had a string of indifferent results and was troubled by his vision. He took the first frame 110-1, but I had a run of good breaks to go 4-3 up. *Snooker Scene* said I looked 'very sharp'. The eighth game was a grinding affair, up and down the table – exactly the sort of frame Ray used to sneak in his best days. But I managed to hold him off to win 5-3.

In the next round Kirk Stevens went two frames up, even though I made a break of 63 in the second. He had his chances to go further ahead, but I laid an impossible snooker to check him and that proved to be the turning-point. I felt a new surge of authority as the winning-post came in sight – the opposite of what I was said to feel in the past – and won the last three frames for the match.

Kirk Stevens was to come to figure in some lurid headlines that season, with the accusation – later sadly confirmed by Kirk himself – that he was a cocaine addict. He always struck me as a rather sad, lonely figure on the circuit, despite his glamorous white suits, his sports car image and his female fan club. He used to play records at the Crucible to soothe him before he went out to play. He always idolised Cliff Thorburn.

His troubles go very deep, back to the night his mother was murdered in Canada. He's an exciting player, much given to flamboyant power shots. He was always very friendly to me. One can only feel sorry for him and hope he comes through his nightmare ordeal.

I was matched against young Neal Foulds in the Rothmans semi-final and 'experience told its tale', as *Snooker Scene* put it later. 'The contest degenerated into an execution as Taylor scored consistently heavily in the balls and Foulds faded to vanishing point.' I went 7-0 up and, although Neal pulled back three frames and produced the shot of the tournament with a touching snooker on the pink with only pink and black remaining, I went through to the final 9-3.

My family noticed that I seemed more relaxed when I was playing. There was less tension when the pressure came on, almost as if the result didn't really matter so much to me as it had in the past. It was an odd phenomenon, obviously a side-effect of my mother's death.

Cliff Thorburn produced a shock result in the other

semi-final, eliminating Steve Davis 9-7 in a classic battle, coming back from 3-6 down. He looked to be in great form and said afterwards: 'I'm a rejuvenated man. I wake up in the mornings looking forward to playing snooker.'

He may have been looking forward to our match but he can't have looked back on it with much pleasure. The semi-final must have drained him because he couldn't reproduce the same form. Not that I gave him much chance. 'Playing like a man possessed,' said *Snooker Scene*, 'Taylor reeled off eight frames in succession for the 10-2 victory which was almost a reversal of the 9-0 drubbing he received from Davis in his last major final on the circuit, the 1981 Jameson International. Taylor was simply devastating.'

I scored a century break of 112, following it with 47 and 49 – that meant I'd scored 208 without reply. 'More important than this mere statistic', said the magazine, 'was the aggression he maintained when holding such a big lead. Earlier in his career, he might well have been more intent on defending it.'

When I finally collected the trophy and the £45,000 cheque – the biggest prize then offered in snooker – the tears started flowing all round. Trish sent Damian up to me from the audience when she saw me filling up and we had an emotional scene.

There were even tears in the press room that night. Janice Hale wrote: 'I have rarely experienced so much feeling during a final. It was hard not to feel that here was a man who had triumphed over so much: grief, bad eyesight, long runs of poor form. Nice guys can come first.'

That was the theme of the editorial in *Snooker Scene*, which I reproduce in full here (with Clive Everton's permission) because it catches, more eloquently than I could describe it myself, that moment of mixed triumph and tragedy in my life:

Dennis Taylor's first major title in his thirteen years as a professional gave the snooker world one of its most memorably emotional evenings. Recognised for so long as a genuine entertainer and a true professional, he became at last a major winner through producing the best snooker of his life.

The 10-2 victory over Cliff Thorburn which gave him the record first prize of £45,000 in the Rothmans Grand Prix came only three weeks after the unexpected death of his mother.

So loved was she that there were two thousand people at her wake in Coalisland. So close-knit and loving is Taylor's family that remains – his father, four sisters, two brothers and his own wife and three children – that his wish to unite them in joy as they had been in sadness transcended any other factor.

Privately still grieving for his mother, taking after the day's match or practice had been completed one or two drinks more than usual, it was a tribute to his self-discipline and professionalism that he was indistinguishable from his usual self in public.

Snooker is a game that requires a high degree of mental clarity, but perhaps because personal tragedy can strengthen the mind's ability to cope with stress, his concentration and mental approach have never been better.

His bereavement also put snooker firmly in perspective. 'I don't think I'll ever feel the pressure that I did in the past. When something like this happens, you realise that snooker comes a poor second to your family,' he said.

Unwelcome as the source of his relief from pressure was, it gave him a positive attitude to the glittering prize which was there for the winning. Neither was he dazzled by the glitter.

In the past, he has met both triumphs, like his two

defeats of Alex Higgins for the Irish title, and disasters, like his 9-0 defeat by Steve Davis in the 1981 Jameson final, with equal grace.

His victory inspired another Kiplingesque reflection: 'If you can keep playing the balls, forget your opponent and forget about the products of winning, then you can be a winner.'

Frequently a player shrivels under another's force of personality or seizes up when victory and its rewards loom tantalisingly close, but Taylor, who has suffered from both maladies in the past, overrode them this time through his irresistible sense of mission.

As psychologically right as any player may be for an important challenge, he cannot win unless his technique is also in prime working order. It should not be forgotten that since Taylor became at ease with his extraordinary Joe 90 spectacles some seven or eight months ago – having adopted them about a year earlier – his form has shown a dramatic improvement.

As a schoolboy, he could not see well enough to read the blackboard but nevertheless so quickly became the best player in Coalisland that often the only way he could get a game at all was to play left-handed. Necessity thus inspired a skill which serves him in his professional career through his ability to play certain shots in this way for which others would be forced to use the rest.

Battling against his blurred vision with unassisted sight, he tried contact lenses – wearing which he reached the 1979 world final – and conventional swivel lens spectacles of the type popularised by Fred Davis and John Pulman. However, it was not until Jack Karneham, not only a coach and BBC commentator but for much of his life a manufacturer of spectacle frames, made a special pair of snooker spectacles for him that he truly began to see the light.

The most important feature of the spectacles are that they are worn so high on the face that a player can look down the cue and through the optical centre of the lens rather than downwards through slight distortion, which is often the case even with conventional swivels. The larger lens area also gives better peripheral vision for pots which are not straight or straightish. 'It looks a different game now,' says Taylor.

Last spring he played outstandingly well to finish second in the Professional Snooker League and went on to reach the semi-finals of the Embassy World Championship. This summer he won the Costa del Sol Classic, not a major event but a first prize nevertheless, and reached the quarter-finals of the Jameson International before his mother's death caused his withdrawal.

His capture of the Rothmans title not only means that he has not lost a match this season, but that the seven ranking points he has accrued from the season's first two ranking tournaments is only one fewer than Steve Davis has earned from his Jameson win and Rothmans semi-final.

A more homely kind of tribute was paid by the local newspaper, *The Democrat*, back in Coalisland. They produced a three-page supplement to mark the victory in which all the local traders took advertisement space to congratulate me. They included the butcher, the baker, the tailor, the hairdresser, the estate agent, the garage, even a Burger bar. My own family put one in saying 'Congratulations Son! We are very proud of your tremendous achievement. Heartiest congratulations. Signed: Daddy, Martin, Brian, Brenda, Molly, Jean, Margaret, Seamus, Malachy, Gerry, Robert and all your nieces and nephews.'

It was just like a parish notice-board – one of the ways

in which a small place like Coalisland can retain a human scale and warmth that are denied to bigger, more anonymous towns where people hardly speak to each other, even when they live next door for most of their lives. My father put in a special note of thanks in which he made the point: 'It is on a joyous occasion like this that you really appreciate the goodness and the quality of the sterling people of Coalisland and the surrounding areas.'

The Democrat also carried a cartoon showing me as a lad in short trousers standing on a lemonade box while Jim-Joe Gervin leans over the table and says: 'Listen here, wee Dennis, if you can't pot that ball Jim-Joe's going to have to buy you a big pair of glasses.'

Why had I suddenly become a winner after being 'one of snooker's also-rans', as I had been described? I've been trying to puzzle it out. The timing of my mother's death couldn't, surely, have been just a coincidence? Trish and my sisters all noticed a change in my approach to the game, so that must have been a relevant factor.

There can be no doubt that the trauma of her death affected my mental attitude to the game in some mysterious way that helped me to win. It was as though some invisible constraint had been broken, some key turned in a lock. People have said that I used to try too hard to win for my mother and that this eagerness seized me up at crucial moments. That is too glib an explanation, for I was never so highly motivated to win as I was after the funeral. My thoughts were constantly going back to the family.

What really happened, I think, is that the enormity of my mother's death put snooker into its proper perspective. It brought home to me the fundamental truth that what really matters in life is life – and that life is about people, especially family and friends. Nothing can be more sacred than that, certainly not a game. I can honestly say that I never thought of the money. As I told *The Times*, 'I've got a family that money can't buy. This is for them and all the folks back home.' This revelation perhaps made me realise who I was and what I wanted from life. That was my mother's legacy, as though the force of her own personality had been passed on to me.

It shouldn't be forgotten, though, that I was already playing well, probably better than ever. I had won the Spanish event and I really felt I was going to win the Jameson before my mother's death made me scratch from the tournament. Two special factors were relevant here: my cue, with which I felt on increasingly good terms, and my glasses.

I had already been quoted as saying of the specs: 'They have made all the difference to my game. I now have the confidence to take on and beat anyone in the world.' Put all three elements into the victory mix and I'll accept the explanation, but none of them on their own is enough.

It was my good fortune that the relaxation in my approach happened to improve my play, perhaps releasing some inner tension that was previously holding me back. For another player it might have had the opposite effect; it might have been disastrous. But that was the way it affected my particular personality. I don't pretend to know why: I'll leave it to others to speculate and quote from Freud if they like. For myself, I simply thank God.

PART FIVE

Top of the World (1985)

'After the Lord Mayor's Show came the dustcart.' That was a fair description of my return to competitive tournament play after ending 1984 on such a high note of personal triumph. Although I beat Warren King, the Australian, 9-5 in the first round of the Coral UK trophy at Preston – with 'soundness, authority and confidence', as one paper put it – I went out head first in the next to Tony Knowles in what was rightly said to be 'an emotionally numb performance'.

It was as though I didn't really care – obviously some reaction to the dramas surrounding my mother's death. Davis thrashed Higgins in the final, reversing the previous year's result. Higgins caught up from 2-8 to 8-9, which must have caused a flutter in the Romford camp, but Steve then rattled off the next seven frames for the match.

Davis was in invincible form. When you are matched against him you take on more than just another snooker player: you are playing both a team and a legend. Steve is reinforced in every possible way by his Romford colleagues. They sit with him at practice, carry his bags, deal with his fan mail, intercept his phone calls, and generally remove from him the basic admin. of life and all the chores that normally entails. He is cossetted from morning to night during a tournament. Either Barry Hearn himself or one of the 'minders', Ron or Robbo, will be with him all the time, either keeping him company at the hotel, walking him to the arena, even jollying him along in the dressing-room back-stage. One can hardly deny that the system seems to work.

The purpose of all this build-up is partly to work on Steve himself, to make him feel special, and partly to work on the opposition, who are made to feel inferior before they even play the first shot. Joe Davis apparently had the same effect on his opponents, according to old Sidney Lee: you were beaten before you started. Steve has the presence to carry this off. He puts space between himself and everybody else. If you're not careful, you find that you're slightly intimidated by the remote glare that comes from his chair.

My immediate opponent, however, was Rex Williams, who put me out in the Mercantile Classic then partnered me in a losing doubles against Virgo and Stevens. Higgins and White won the Hofmeister doubles easily against Thorburn and Thorne, having really won the tournament in the semi-final by defeating the Romford holders, Davis and Meo. Higgins is always formidable in doubles. Jimmy White has more natural ability than any player in the game, but he should have done more with it than he has. He has the ability and the temperament, so his tactical game must be faulty somewhere. He needs to work out for himself where he's going wrong and adapt his game slightly. He doesn't need to do much, as he's very tough to beat already.

Willie Thorne's victory in the Mercantile Credit at Warrington gave great pleasure to everyone in the game – not least to Racing Raymond and the other loyal Leicester punters who have staked a fortune on him over the years. As so often, the real victory was over Steve

Davis in the semi-final, where Willie confounded us all with his fighting spirit. He had never been nearer than 3-9 down to Davis in a competition before. Steve blew it with a hard-hit green to the centre pocket which stayed out when he might have played safe. Willie's final with Thorburn produced some marvellous snooker, including three centuries in a single evening session. The champagne corks were popping till dawn. Willie must have been pleased to wash the champagne down with the thought that he had finally silenced critics who say he lacks 'bottle'.

Cliff didn't wait long to find consolation, winning the Benson and Hedges Masters over Mountjoy. The winner also eliminated yours truly in the first round. This helped me to maintain my unenviable record of never having won a match in this tournament in eight appearances. It must be London that doesn't suit me.

I certainly didn't like the Wembley audience, which was noisy, ignorant and bad-mannered. They applauded bad shots because they didn't know any better. Alex was their hero. He got himself into trouble when he beat Davis by going to the rougher elements in the crowd and mouthing some bad language that was picked up on the television screen. I've been told that the Masters will have more discipline next time – I hope so, because it couldn't go on the way it was. It was unfair on the players and on the better behaved parts of the audience. There is no room for football-type hooliganism in a game like snooker that was bred on hush.

After a first round exit in the Tolly Cobbold I reached the quarter-final of the Dulux tournament at Derby, going down to Kirk Stevens. This was the event at which Kirk, who lost in the final to Silvino Francisco, became the centre of the drug sensation.

I had a chance to take immediate revenge on Kirk when I beat him for Ireland against Canada in the

Guinness World Cup. The Irish team of Alex Higgins, Eugene Hughes and myself beat England, led by Steve Davis, in the final. I always take a special pride in these international events and I have to confess that I once shed tears in the dressing-room when I lost a game for Ireland.

Tears would have been redundant on this occasion, for I didn't lose a match. I was relieved to force a draw with Tony Knowles in the final after he had gone one frame and 64 points up, and I potted a memorable long black in my game against Davis. But the Irish hero on this occasion was undoubtedly Alex, who turned a 5-7 deficit into a 9-7 triumph by taking four inspired frames in succession against Meo and Davis.

The fact that I have played representative snooker for England as an amateur and for Ireland as a professional highlights the split in my national personality. In this respect I am like thousands of other Irishmen, especially those from the North. I have lived almost equal amounts of my life in each country. My parents were Irish and my wife and children were all born and brought up in England. I feel I am part of both countries and that both are now part of me

But my roots, of course, are in Ireland and it is in Irish humour that I seem to find my most natural form of expression. Never more so than when I meet up with my golfing chum Frank Carson, the comedian, who always has me snookered at this style of native wit.

Here's Carson on my glasses: 'He needed to win that world title for the £60,000 when you think how much he spends on Windolene. With those glasses he's the nearest thing to the front of a Ford Cortina. He must have good eyesight to see through them. I'll let you into a secret. Those glasses make the pockets look bigger and the balls smaller.'

My own favourite comment on my glasses came from

Eddie Charlton, a man not normally known for his wit: he said I looked like Mickey Mouse with a welding shield on.

Carson on my victory: 'Since Dennis walked off with the winner's cheque the value of the pound has risen and his bank manager has moved to larger premises. He cashed a cheque and the bank bounced. The win has made him very conceited: he's going to night school to learn how to spell his name.'

On my brief boxing career: 'He was the only boxer in Northern Ireland to sell advertising space on the soles of his shoes. He was once so far behind on points he needed a knock-out for a draw.'

One joke I use in my own routine is about a man who complains to his doctor that he doesn't feel well and confesses to a diet of snooker balls.

'How many do you eat?'

'I have two reds and a brown for breakfast, a blue and a pink for lunch and three reds and a black for dinner.'

'Well, there's your problem – you're not getting enough greens.'

The finale of my exhibitions is a trick shot in which a volunteer comes forward from the audience, usually a pretty girl, and lies on her back on the table. I place a piece of chalk in her mouth and balance the black ball on it like a golf tee. I then knock the ball off the chalk on to the table and into a far pocket. Once I had a male volunteer who had no teeth to hold the chalk in.

While I'm setting up this trick I tell the audience jokes to fill the silence. I was the first snooker player to stand up and tell jokes as opposed to exchanging light banter with the audience. One joke is that a volunteer swallowed the ball. After a pause I add: 'You should have seen the shot I had to play to get the black out of there.'

Telling Irish jokes in Ireland is always, of course, a bit of a problem. The Irish don't seem to feel insulted, but I'm sometimes a bit embarrassed myself. I used to be careful about making jokes about Alex Higgins among his own folk in Belfast, but they now know him so well they don't mind.

Carson says of Alex: 'Someone threw a petrol bomb at him – and Alex drank it. When Alex and I play golf together I always warn him: "Don't lean over or you'll spill." '

Alex was my next opponent in the Irish championship, sponsored by Strongbow, at the Ulster Hall in Belfast. I was glad to regain the title. This is always a satisfying one to win, but this time there were two additional grounds for satisfaction. The margin was a convincing one of 10-5 – and I had run into top form just a few days before the World Championships were due to start at the Crucible Theatre in Sheffield.

There is nothing to beat the Crucible atmosphere. It is partly the shape of the theatre, which has steeply banked seating that draws the spectators' attention hypnotically down to the tables, as to an altar in church. It is partly, of course, the blanket coverage on the BBC, which builds up the event to a thrilling climax by involving the viewers in every stage of the play, encouraging them to select their own heroes and villains as the plot unfolds.

Embassy's back-stage organisation is also superb, and the prizes are such that it remains the tournament everybody wants to win – the big one, the pot of pots, the event to which the whole season's efforts are directed, the one that finally settles all doubts. You can lose everything else all season and still be the champion if you pull this one off. Even if you have won everything else already, it counts for nothing after Sheffield.

After two first-round knock-outs when I turned professional, I had maintained a good record in this tournament – one final and three semi-finals. People had forecast that I would win it by the age of thirty. Now I was thirty-six. Perhaps my time had come. I certainly rated my chances higher than the bookies did. They were offering 40-1 on me and 10-1 on Higgins, even though I had just beaten him 10-5 for the Irish title.

My first game was played in the full glare of publicity, because my opponent, Silvino Francisco, had accused Kirk Stevens in that morning's *Daily Star* of being 'as high as a kite on dope'. The headlines were almost as high themselves, and the Press arrived in their droves, which must have put Silvino under pressure.

I put him under pressure, too, with breaks of 54, 67, 40, 50, 92 and 128 to beat him 10-2. Two years before we had had a much closer match when I won the last three frames to pip him at the post. But Silvino's mind was on other things this time. He denied that he'd said the things attributed to him by the paper and offered an apology to Kirk. The players were as baffled as everyone else at this turn of events, which got even more confusing later when Kirk returned to Toronto and admitted that the drug accusations were true anyway.

In the next round I met Eddie Charlton, who struggled back from 1-4 down to 5-6, but I then left him behind to run away 13-6. Eddie never gives up, but he missed some important balls in this match, including a last red which might have brought him level at 6-6.

The next round, I knew, would be crucial. Cliff Thorburn has always been my toughest opponent and he would be thirsting for revenge after the drubbing I gave him in the final of the Rothmans Grand Prix. I knew I had to match him in safety play, which promised a long, slow grinding affair – for which my game against 'Steady Eddie' had at least been a useful warm-up.

In the event, the match lasted ten hours, one session ending at 1.21 a.m., which made me no friends in the press room. Cliff said afterwards: 'I wasn't the only one who played safe. If I'd played well this would have been the longest match ever.' I went four frames up, but that means nothing against Thorburn, and I had to play him at his own game, matching him all day in tactics and concentration, to win 13-5. Cliff said later: 'He had an answer to everything I tried.' I thought I'd cheer up the press boys after keeping them up so late, and told them my taxi-fare had been £2.50 but I only had £2 in my wallet – so I'd asked the driver to reverse a bit!

After beating Cliff I felt quietly confident and ready for anything. Evidently Barry Hearn was heard to say in the press room that I might turn out to be the man for Steve to beat in the final. I hadn't time to think as far ahead as that since I was needed in Dublin to make a TV commercial for King's Crisps!

I returned to face Tony Knowles in the semi-final after he had knocked out Jimmy White in a high-scoring match. Tony had made a break of 137 which might have been 144 – and thus one ahead of Bill Werbeniuk – if he hadn't missed a thin cut on the final black. That cost him £6,000 – which adds up to a great many cans of lager for Big Bill, who can dispose of twenty or more a day.

This was bound to be a totally different tactical game from the one against Thorburn, since Tony likes to go for his shots. He had evidently decided that I might be tired after the Thorburn marathon and went into the attack, going 2-0 up straightaway. He had a chance to make it three, but I scrambled back with a break of 45, drew level in the fourth frame with an 83, then went ahead with 117. Overnight I was leading 10-5.

Tony tends to throw his cue at the ball when things are going against him, instead of quietly working out where he's going wrong and correcting it. He seemed to get angry with himself, unable to understand why he couldn't reproduce the form he had shown against Jimmy White. He sat slumped in his chair looking cross while I chatted to the audience.

132

He looked even crosser the next day, but not with himself or even with me. He blamed the lights and asked for a special seat to be brought in to the arena so that he didn't have to sit under a particular spotlight. This is such a well-organised event, with everything possible done for the players' ease and comfort, that this struck me as ridiculous. Impishly, I couldn't resist making a joke of it. I asked Paul Hatherell, the tournament director, to make sure Tony was comfortable. Would he like an armchair – or perhaps a three-piece suite? I added that I'd have liked an armchair myself during my long match with Thorburn. The audience loved it, but Tony couldn't raise a smile. He rarely does. If I'd been cheeky enough, I would have suggested that they got him a double bed, in the light of his well-publicised amorous adventures.

What Tony couldn't acknowledge was that on the day I was able to out-pot him. His vanity wouldn't allow him to accept that. But it was true – and I was delighted. Tony was a bit ungracious in defeat, I thought – though I can understand his disappointment. To beat Steve, he said, I'd need to play as well as that again, get the run of the ball and have a lot of luck besides. Who was to say I wouldn't? I was interested to hear David Taylor, the 'Silver Fox', say after his match against Davis that he thought the champion might be vulnerable if somebody could stay with him and exploit some holes in his game.

I'd already heard that Steve had been cueing badly just before this event at the Benson and Hedges Irish Masters and had gone to the Blackpool guru, Frank Callan, for treatment. Steve is always obsessed with technique and has even been known to change his action in the middle of a tournament. He and Frank Callan both believe that the secret lies in the pause at the back of the stroke before making impact on the cue-ball. This is something I've had to think about a lot, since Clive Everton has accused me of snatching under pressure.

I don't think you can be dogmatic about these things. Gary Owen, who won the world amateur title twice, just flicked the cue, so that every shot was a snatch. It was the way he played the game and he played it very well. Cliff Thorburn hardly brings the cue back at all. He just gives a short stab at the ball, but he can still play deep power shots. Terry Griffiths used to go so far back from the ball when he paused that he increased the margin of error on contact.

I used to work out that I needed to hold the cue tighter, but that was a mistake. I remember John Pulman saying to me in the early days that it was important to get the last pause right and this would stop the snatch. He thought a little bit of snatch didn't matter if the contact action was right. He thought I had a terrific contact action on the lines of Joe Davis's. Steve has a lovely cueing action but he does worry about it a lot.

In the press conference after my match with Knowles I had joked that it wouldn't be so easy against Davis – maybe 16-6 instead of 16-5. But I'd had the grace to roar with laughter as I said it. I knew it wouldn't be as easy as that. Steve had beaten me in eight of our nine encounters – though the score was only 2-1 in the World Championship. On the other hand, I calculated that I had lost only 18 frames on my way to the final and he had lost 22.

The bookies naturally favoured Steve and so did the press, though Jean Rook, the self-styled First Lady of Fleet Street, cheered me with her friendly forecast: 'He is totally honest; utterly lovable and, in the unlikely event of his winning the crown, he could turn out like King George VI – the king who came from the back to prove himself one of the most popular in recent history.' Mind you, I've no idea what she knows about snooker. She called me the King of Clubs and Steve the King of Diamonds. 'Snooker kings are adored like royalty', she said, 'by the hushed crowds they can silence with a sceptre-style wave of a cue. They're served by white-gloved attendants in scarlet livery. Every move they make on TV holds up the breath of millions who hesitate to cough, even in their own armchairs. But a snooker table isn't round, and only one man can finally stand, conqueror, at its head.'

To most of the press it was the Robot versus the Joker. Graham Nickless in the *Daily Star* said I would give snooker 'a shot in the arm' and had 'brought the smile back into a game blackened by the drug scandal'. He quoted me as saying: 'Yes, I will carry on smiling and keep my sense of humour whatever happens, because it is still only a game after all. I am enjoying my snooker more now than I have for years.'

Hugh McIlvanney in *The Observer* said he had a 'frail hope' that I would win:

Steve Davis has cast himself so convincingly as an executioner that when Dennis Taylor walked into the Crucible Theatre, Sheffield, some of the audience almost expected the Irishman to dispense with his extravagant glasses and call for a blindfold.

Their gloomy predictions owed much to the assumption that the qualities which make Taylor a mature and attractive man in a game where adolescence can last to the brink of middle age would weigh heavily against him in the greatest test of his career. As he looks out amiably on the world through enough glass to front a small shop, he finds no trouble in persuading himself that there is life beyond snooker, that his dedication to it should come a long way behind commitment to his family for a start.

Against Davis, perhaps the deadliest amalgam of technical and psychological resources snooker has known, such a human sense of perspective could be seen as a handicap. In this corner at least, the match began with the frail hope that Taylor would remind us that even in an anti-Corinthian era, warm, humorous, well-rounded and civilised natures can sometimes go all the way to the big prizes in the most mercenary of arenas.

I'd been struck by an interview Steve gave to *Woman* magazine. 'If I had to choose between sex and snooker,' he said, 'I'd have to choose snooker. Snooker is my justification, my fulfilment.' I had come to exactly the opposite conclusion. My personal fulfilment was in my family. Snooker was just a way of earning a living. I wondered which of these attitudes would be most help once the chips were down.

The difference in our approaches to the game showed in the way we were living in Sheffield. Steve had the Cadillac and the whole Romford supporting cast, with people to carry his cue, answer his letters and his telephone calls, order his breakfast, polish his shoes. I had Trish in my corner, with a relieving column of family and friends on their way over from Coalisland. Trish and I just pottered about the hotel, ringing home from time to time to see how the kids were. I also had Walt Floyd, a snooker fan from Barrow who had become a good friend and actually designed our new house on the hill by the golf course on the edge of Blackburn, into which we moved three years ago. Walt was an old friend of Ray Reardon and once shared rooms with him. We are always pleased to visit his nightclub at Barrow. And there was always the cheery support of Trevor East, the ITV sports producer, who had always shown great faith in me, both as a player and a commentator, and had become a pal I could trust.

The build-up back-stage at the Crucible is suitably theatrical, with wires and cables and scaffolding and signs saying 'Band Room' and 'Green Room' and 'Quick Change Room' to add to the showbiz atmosphere. We are interviewed in the dressing-room these days like footballers at a Cup Final and then make the long walk to the back of the stage and wait while the introductions are made. Then, when our name is called, we go through the orange curtains into the arena like the gladiators of old. It's a very strange moment as you blink at the bright lights, register the crowd, catch sight of the TV cameras and realise that millions of people are watching. There's no way back, no hiding place, and you're out there on your own, more lonely than you've felt in your life. I now know what Steve meant when he said that 'your soul is out there for everybody to see – it's a kind of nightmare'.

It was soon a nightmare for me. I had a good chance in the first frame after opening with a 50 break, but I missed the last red to the middle pocket and Steve cleaned up. Then he made 87. The third frame was crucial and tense, but I lost it after some nervous safety play. I had a chance in the fourth but overcut a red. Steve's length was immaculate, judged to an inch, the shots nestling on the baulk cushion, leaving me nothing to play with. I kept my spirits up with the odd joke. On one occasion, when I was already hopelessly behind, Steve elected to roll up behind the yellow for a tight snooker instead of trying the pot. 'I've got him worried,' I said. But by the end of the first session I was 0-7 down. The 9-0 whitewash Steve gave me at the Jameson in 1981 was on everybody's mind – I tried to keep it out of mine.

After the interval I lost another frame by the huge margin of 121-0 to go 0-8 down. By this time I wasn't feeling too great, as you can imagine, but I was more embarrassed than anything. I had been in such good form all week that I knew it was bound to return. But when – would it be too late?

I must have looked a sorry sight. Hugh McIlvanney

said I was 'painful to behold':

> Red-faced and seeming to sink ever lower than his
> chair, looking more and more like a sick owl resigned to
> being savaged by an eagle, he was humiliated beyond
> anything a nice man should be asked to suffer. Davis
> was parading the full chilling authority of his genius
> and the irrevocability of the plot became more blatant
> with every pot he made, every elementary blunder his
> unnerved opponent perpetrated.

When I finally won a frame, the ninth, it was about 8.15
in the evening – over six hours since we had started. It
had taken me about forty minutes in this session to pot a
single ball. But at last I was on my way, and I could feel
the cue-action functioning again, like a car that has been
on choke after a damp start and is suddenly running
smoothly. I resisted the temptation to grip the cue more
tightly and concentrated on keeping my head still. In the
interval Trish reminded me how well I'd played against
Thorburn and said I was bound to make a comeback.

Even though Steve went to 9-1 with a break of 57, I
knew it was only a matter of time before my turn came. I
remember that a TV camera squeaked behind me just as
I was bending to play. I paused, then got up and went
over to the camera and made as if to oil it with my cue.
The crowd roared with laughter. The incident seemed to
release some tension all round and I went on to make a
break of 61. More than that, I played 'like a man
possessed', according to *Snooker Scene*, and took five
frames in a row, including a break of 98. I thought there
might be a maximum on, so I tried a risky plant to the
middle pocket to stay on the black – which shows how
relaxed I must have been feeling.

I was encouraged by the fact that Steve wasn't taking
on possible pots but playing safe instead, which

suggested that I had gained the initiative. It was now 6-9 and the last frame of the evening was clearly crucial – I would either go to bed 7-9 or 6-10 down, which is quite a difference. I remembered blowing a similar chance against Terry Griffiths in the final of 1979. This time, after a great deal of cat-and-mouse play, I came from behind with the help of a vicious snooker on the brown and an in-off by Steve and won with a slow agonising pink for the frame.

The crowd went wild with excitement as the pink went down. They knew there was a match on now. So did Steve. I caught sight of his face, stiff as a mask, as we walked off. The memory I had triggered off in his mind was that famous defeat by Alex Higgins in the UK Coral trophy, when he squandered a 7-0 lead. Now it had happened again: he had nearly lost leads of 8-0 and 9-1. Looking back, that late surge on the Saturday evening was crucial, because Steve could never feel safe again. No matter how far ahead he might get round the final bend, he would be listening for my tread over his shoulder. I knew which of us would sleep better that night.

Trish and I no longer felt so isolated now, with all the friendly, familiar faces from Coalisland coming round to wish us well. Three of my sisters had also come over with their husbands and my brother Martin was there. We were amused to see that some of the Sunday papers had been unable to catch up with my late run the night before and had virtually buried me for dead. Trish much preferred to be at the tournaments with me rather than worrying about it at home and having to guess my mood from the telephone. A tournament becomes such a closed world, especially the Crucible, that you need people there with you. I felt surrounded by warm and friendly support. I just hoped I wouldn't let these people down.

I went to mass on Sunday morning at St Marie's Cathedral, across the road from the Crucible, with Trish and Denise and two of my sisters. It wasn't so much to seek divine help – I thought He had already worked overtime the night before – but because we would normally go. My mother and my aunts had all been regular attenders and Trish and I just carried on. No matter what your religion is, it's nice to have one. Even at mass a man stepped out of the congregation to shake hands and the priest said at the end: 'We welcome our Irish guests and wish them all the best this afternoon.'

My winning streak extended to seven frames in the afternoon when I won the first game, with a break of 53, just failing to tip the last red off the cushion. But I then let two slip away to go 8-11 down. In one of these I missed the last red when it was only inches from the pocket, but I was relieved to see Steve miss a straight brown and then a frame-ball pink with the rest. I got the pink with the half-butt, but unfortunately I missed the half-ball black from the spot and left it on.

Steve sat a long time in his chair, took a sip of water, wiped his hands, then came out to cut the black in. Although I was three frames behind, I wasn't too disheartened, even after losing a black-ball game, since Steve had shown himself to be capable of missing straightforward shots. He definitely wasn't in one of his unbeatable moods. I had to stick close to him and keep the pressure on.

This seemed to work in the next frame, an edgy one full of safety play, because Steve made several misses. Breaks of 48, 57 and 55 put me level at 11-all, which almost brought the house down. But Steve stopped the rot in the next by coming from 50 behind, then took another black-ball game to finish the session at 13-11. I felt I was a bit unlucky to have played so well in the afternoon and yet still be two frames behind. I'd been ahead in every frame but one, and even that one I won. Champions win frames even when they're not playing well. Steve was going to be a hard man to beat.

I felt this even more strongly as he took the opening frame of the evening to go three ahead again. The next one was vital and I nearly blew it, banging the reds around and leaving him a whole cherry orchard to pick from. But he let me in for a 61. I could feel the tension in him, but I was determined not to allow it to affect me. At one point, when I left an easy red on, I said: 'I'm trying to tempt him into a pot here!' When there was a lot of squeaking back-stage I stopped and called: 'Quasimodo?'

I'm sure this helped – it certainly helped me to stay loose and not let his mood dominate me. Somebody said to me afterwards that my ability to make jokes when he was so uptight gave me a psychological advantage as the evening wore on. It made him feel that here was a man with something to spare, that I'd keep coming back and wouldn't allow his will to break mine, as it had broken so many others before, including my own.

It helped that the crowd were on my side. I could sense the wave of popular feeling in the Crucible that was wishing me on. This must have made things harder for Steve. His image is one of such cold efficiency that the crowds don't warm to him as much as they do to his opponent. This is a very British characteristic – wanting the champion to be proved vulnerable and the underdog to win.

There was an interval at 13-15, which helped to buoy me up. David Vine came back-stage for an interview in the dressing-room, so there was no time to brood. I came straight back out to make 57 and 79 and go level 15-all. The crowd erupted with excitement. But it was as if I'd exhausted myself with the effort of pulling back to level terms and then let my guard slip for a moment. You can't do that with a man like Davis around.

At 15-17 my position was pretty desperate – he needed only one frame for the match. There was no margin for error. I had to gather myself for the supreme effort. When Steve nipped out for a short break I went too and signalled to Trevor East to follow me from the press benches. His cheery banter and his honest uncomplicated belief in me were what I needed now. He was one of the few people I could feel relaxed with.

Steve got in early in the next one and made 25. One of the worst things for the sitting-out player is that you are below the level of the table. You're sitting there full of anxiety, desperately hoping you'll get another chance, but you can't quite see the balls. The audience and the millions of people watching on television can see much better than I can. I have to force myself not to stand up and watch. Finally Steve missed a straight brown across the table, straining for position on the blue. It was an incredible miss and we both knew it. I made 42, ending with a really tough snooker. At this point Brenda's husband in the audience let out a whistle of relief, and referee John Williams nearly ordered him out.

All the drama was on the last red. I got a chance along the cushion, but I stretched too far and left it on. Incredibly, Steve then left it on the edge of the pocket. He stared down on the shot in disbelief. I got the red and the yellow but missed the green. Steve got it but missed the brown. I potted the brown along the length of the table, but missed the blue. Steve left a long blue on for me, which I got. All on the pink, which I slotted slowly into the middle. I took a deep breath as the crowd rose to their feet in joyful relief.

It was still sudden death for me – and I thought it had arrived when I left a red on for Steve. But he missed it to gasps all round. I got it and cut in a very difficult black, then went on to 57. The frame ended scrappily but I had made it: 17-all. Not for a decade, not since Reardon beat Charlton in Australia, had the World Championship gone to a last-frame decider. By this time it was after 11 p.m.

and virtually the whole of Britain was looking on. I have hardly met a person since who wasn't following every shot.

My sisters told me later they were hardly able to watch. Margaret, the youngest, didn't watch at all. She looked away from the table throughout and called on our late mother to guide the balls into the hole. When Steve was lining up a shot she said: 'He won't get it because Mummy won't let him get it!' Brenda had wanted to go out for a smoke at the interval, but Trish had said: 'You can't leave him now.' Over in Dungannon my Aunt Molly had fallen off a cardboard box in her excitement.

I took an early lead in the final frame but the balls were awkwardly placed along the top cushion. It wasn't going to be easy to clear them. We were in for a long haul. I began to sink in my chair when Steve took the lead going into the colours, but he couldn't get the yellow and snookered me on it. I then tried to double the yellow and left it on. I thought the fates were against me when Steve fluked the green to go 62-44 ahead. That meant I was 18 behind with a possible 22 on the table. But I needed all the colours – brown, blue, pink and black – while Steve needed only one.

Afterwards *Snooker Scene* was to say of this situation: 'It was a time for bravery; it was a time for caution; it was a time for hope; it was a time for fear'. I certainly felt all four emotions in rapid succession as I looked at the brown. We both missed it twice as the crowd sat on the edge of their seats, hardly daring to breathe. Then I'm faced with an awkward shot as the cue-ball lies close to the cushion. The brown was also near the side cushion at the other end of the table. The pot was possibly on, but I shouldn't really have risked it from that position at that stage of the match. On the other hand, there was no easy safety shot either. If I'd gone for safety I might have kissed the blue and let Steve in. I decided to have a go and my heart danced with relief as the brown disappeared. By now the crowd were applauding every shot. The cheer that went up after the brown almost lifted the roof off – I think people sensed that that was the key to unlock the rest.

But it's never a formality under this pressure. The blue had been nudged towards the other baulk pocket when I potted the brown, which made the angle more acute, but I cut it in. The cue-ball was again fairly tight on the cushion for the pink, more so than I had intended. Again there was no safety shot so I went for it, down it went. I staggered over to the trophy on its stand with a shaky hand as if to say: 'So near and yet so far!' I don't know what made me do that at such a tense moment in the game. I had already set up a double on the black into the centre pocket as I sank the pink, and I knew it was now or never.

In fact we were to have seven shots at the black in what must be the greatest finale of any snooker match. I thought there would only be one when the crowd gave a great roar as my attempted double seemed to be going in. I couldn't see and relied on the crowd to tell me. It was a cruel moment when the black hit the jaws of the centre pocket. Fortunately, it rebounded to safety on the top cushion while the cue-ball went behind the baulk-line.

Steve then played a finely judged safety shot which reversed the position of the two balls. I cheekily tried to double it into the top pocket, while ensuring that there would be distance between the cue-ball and the black if I missed. I didn't play it perfectly, and the black just crept past the centre pocket. That was three shots.

There was nothing really on for Steve and he would normally have gone for a safety shot. In fact, most commentators thought that's what he was trying, but he has since told me he was attempting a double into the top pocket with the chance of a 'cocked hat' into the centre

144

pocket if it missed. I must have psyched him into this by going for two doubles myself. It is a crazy way to try to win a World Championship. You have to put a lot of faith in the cushions to hit a perfect double, and it is very hard to go safe because of the risk of a rebound from the jaws of the pocket. Steve knew that very well and wouldn't normally have considered it. In the event, he missed and got a double-kiss which let me in with a chance.

That should have been the end because I had a long three-quarter pot to the baulk pocket with the balls comfortably close together. It wasn't a certainty by any means, especially under these circumstances, but I should have got it all the same. When I missed it and saw both balls going back down the table I didn't even look any more. I put my head down and walked in misery to my chair. I'd had my chance and I'd missed it.

It was only when I got to the chair and peered across the table that I realised Steve's shot wasn't a formality. I had screwed the cue-ball close to the side cushion, hampering his shot, and the black was just an inch or two further away from the hole than he would have liked. It occurred to me that I'd been a bit lucky when I missed my pot. If I'd hit the jaws I might have left an easier shot on. It was a finely angled cut. He'd have to hit down on the cue-ball because of the cushion and he'd have to watch the target ball very carefully to hit it at the right angle. This meant that the pocket wouldn't be in his line of vision as he played the shot. It wasn't actually as easy a shot as the one I'd just missed.

Even so, I expected him to get it. As he said himself afterwards, he would have got it seven times out of ten. I couldn't watch as he played it, but I knew he'd missed when a great gasp and then a cheer went up from the crowd. He'd left it on – and thankfully close to the pocket. As I rose from my chair for the last time I remembered a thought that had come into my head earlier: 'The worst thing that can happen to you tonight, Dennis Taylor, is that you'll win £35,000.' I sank it – and the reward for that one shot went up by £25,000.

Money was the last thing on my mind, however. I wanted to flee with my family and whoop it up. I waved to Trish and she came down from the audience and kissed me. But we're shy people, not given to public display. She just nestled against my arm. I waved a finger at Trevor East and learned afterwards that he had backed me at 40-1. He deserved it after the faith he had always shown in me.

David Vine stuck a microphone straight under Steve's nose as he sat shattered in his chair, looking more broken than I've ever seen a man, the thought of that missed cut burning in his brain. David had his job to do, but it was cruel for Steve. Some people didn't like his response, but I thought he did well for a man whose nerves must have been red raw. 'Can you believe what just happened out there!' said David.

'You've just seen it – in black and white,' said Steve.

There was a press conference, at which I learned that the *Irish Times* had stopped their presses for the first time in their history to wait for the result. My journalist friends and I just grinned at each other. There wasn't much to say and we were all exhausted. 'A bit of a match that,' I said finally.

The sponsors threw a party in the arena and I stood in a daze with a glass of champagne in my hand accepting congratulations from people I scarcely knew. We finally got the family together and tumbled into a minibus. The journey back to the Hotel St George was magic. We were on our own at last. We could sing Irish songs and pop champagne corks in sheer joy. When we got to the hotel one of my sisters shut the door to her room and burst out crying.

We all came down to drinks in the music lounge. I'd

been trying to ring Dad in Coalisland and finally got through to hear of the riotous celebrations going on over there. There was no question of anybody going to bed here either. Everybody had been through such tension they just had to let off steam. Bruce Donkin of Riley's had thrown a party that had got into full swing in the hotel and a photographer came over and persuaded Trish and myself to do the hokey-cokey.

We grabbed a short sleep before the media pack came round wanting to film us eating breakfast. The telephone was ringing non-stop with messages of support. One was from my old friends Barbara and Cliff Thorburn. Barbara had come over from Canada hoping to see Cliff in the final but she still had the grace to ring me to express their genuine delight at my win. Even though there is rivalry in snooker there is still a great spirit of sportsmanship.

It was only afterwards that I realised what it had meant to all the people watching. There had been 18.5 million viewers tuned in to the final, a new record for any sporting event. Electricity grids had had to carry a higher load than ever before after midnight. Everybody seemed to want to relive every moment, which was why I kept being asked on to TV programmes to take them through it again. Terry Wogan had me on his programme twice in successive weeks, which had never happened before.

What had made the final so special, I think, was not just the almost unbearable tension of the 'sudden death' on the black, but my fight back from so far behind. There was also the fact that we were both so beautifully cast in our respective roles.

Steve was the champion, the tall, silent executioner – one writer described him as a Japanese Samurai. I was Mr Everyman, the cheeky underdog, daring to topple the king. 'It was like Sergeant Bilko beating Ali over the full 15,' Frank Keating wrote in the *Guardian*.

It was the purest sporting theatre, culminating in a

more dramatic climax than anyone could have invented. And it should not be forgotten that Steve's role was every bit as vital as mine. Furthermore, he knew how it felt to be the winner, which can't have made losing any easier to bear.

I have now won one world final and lost another. Mae West used to say 'I've been rich and I've been poor – and believe me, honey, rich is best.' Well, I've been a winner and I've been a loser – and believe me, honey, winning's best.

The first big decision for me after Sheffield was to put my business affairs in order. It was already clear after the Rothmans tournament that Trish couldn't cope any longer with arranging my schedule and settling my fees while running a home and three children at the same time. The telephone calls were non-stop from people wanting my services. It wasn't fair on Trish to have to explain that my charges were now much higher – especially to people we had known for years.

Trish and I have always had to be careful. We're not likely to start splashing out now. We'll always expect value for money. We may move house again, but we'll stay in the same area because that's where the children are rooted and Blackburn has always been kind to us. However busy my work schedule is, I'll always insist on spending a good deal of time with the family because that's the way I am. But it requires good staff work to achieve that, and we obviously needed the best professional help available.

I had already made an approach to Barry Hearn, because I admired his way of conducting business. Some people find Barry brash about money, but he has done a great deal to increase the rewards for everyone in the game. Besides, I like his style of humour and his directness. You always know where you are. He was already looking after Terry Griffiths and Tony Meo, as well as Steve Davis, and he found that quite enough to get on with. But after the Rothmans he had agreed to talk to me again during the summer, when I would anyway be going with the Romford boys on their Far East tour.

After the World Championship Trevor East spoke to Barry, setting out the advantages of a new arrangement, and when we met there was little for us to do but shake hands on it. My friendship with Terry was a help and I fitted in easily with the others. Steve has always admired my comic performances at exhibitions – and perhaps by now he'd come to admire my snooker too!

I've certainly been kept busy enough since. Here is a diary of one week's work to give an idea of what a snooker pro's life can be like. It was compiled in long-hand by Eugene Crozier, who looked after me on Barry's behalf when I returned to Ireland six weeks after the World Championship. This is exactly as he wrote it:

AN EXTRAORDINARY BUSY WEEK FOR DENNIS TAYLOR

TUESDAY 18 JUNE

11.00	Dennis Taylor arrives at Dublin Airport. Eugene Crozier and Jimmy Kinsella, organisers of the tour, are there to greet him in the V.I.P. lounge. Dennis receives a very warm welcome from Don Tracey, Sean, Una and Brenda of the airport staff.
11.50	Dennis, Eugene and Jimmy set off to Guinness brewery.
12.30	Dennis arrives at the brewery and is met by Guinness directors, where he is brought to a private luncheon in the board dining-room. He

	is presented by a director with a Dublin crystal tankard.
1.45	Dennis is then brought on a tour of the brewery, where he meets about 150-200 employees.
2.15	Dennis is then moved to the hopstore, where he meets Jimmy Magee, who runs over the format of questions for the media event.
2.45	Jimmy Magee takes the rostrum and introduces Dennis to an audience of 200 people, Guinness staff and press.
3.30	Dennis does his trick shots.
3.50	Media photographs and interviews.
4.30	Dennis does not have time to check into his hotel, but would like to have a shower. Eugene leaves without Dennis and sets off to a private house across the way and is mobbed by about eighty young fans who want to see Dennis play. Eugene quickly gets into the car and gives the eighty young fans a ride on his car.
4.50	Dennis has had a shower and is ready for 'OFF' on a whirlwind tour of Guinness pubs. Eugene at this time has the car parked back at the brewery and the luggage changed into the limo.
5.00	Gerry Neville hosts the tour and the limo is off.
5.25	Dennis and company arrive at the Finglass Inn. He is greeted by about a thousand fans and a dog who gets in his way on his return to the limo.
5.50	Second appearance: The Towers, Ballymun. 300 fans.
6.15	Third appearance: The Penthouse, Ballymun. 500-600 fans. A young priest arrives on the scene and wants Dennis to open his new social hall. Eugene explains this is impossible and asks him to step in and have his photo taken

with Dennis to hang in his hall.

6.45   Fourth appearance at the Black Sheep northside shopping centre, 300 fans. Dennis is greeted by a kissogram and signs autographs.

7.10   Dennis and Eugene check into the Burlington Hotel. Dennis likes the presidential suite and goes for a swim in the pool.

8.00   Departure from the hotel.

8.25   Fifth appearance: the Beavers Ballinteer, 600-700 fans. Dennis and company meet the proprietor, who has tea and sandwiches laid on. Dennis pauses for some photos, says a few words, etc.

8.50   The limo leaves for the next visit via country roads.

9.05   Sixth appearance at the Noggin Inn, Sallynoggin, 400-500 fans. Dennis meets Jimmy Long, ex-Irish amateur champion. This is the place where Eugene Hughes started his career.

9.30   Seventh appearance at the Golden Ball, Kilternan, 400 fans. Dennis officially opens the snooker room and buys a drink for everybody.

10.05   Eighth appearance at Bray, 300-400 fans. The red carpet is laid for Dennis and he meets the Lord Mayor and champagne is served. Dennis is interviewed by the local radio. The interviewer asks the questions but doesn't listen to the answers. Eugene helps Dennis to shake hands.

10.30   Ninth appearance at Vevay Inn, Bray, 500 fans. Dennis and company arrive by Garda escort (whom we lose at one point on the way when he turns left and we go straight on). Dennis signs autographs etc.

11.00   The day has finally ended, so Dennis, Eugene,

Jimmy and Bernard Gibbons go to a Chinese restaurant for a meal.

1.45   Jimmy goes home and Bernard leaves Dennis and Eugene at the hotel.

WEDNESDAY 19 JUNE

6.45   Eugene gets up and takes a taxi to Guinness brewery and collects his car.

8.45   Dennis and Eugene have breakfast in the room.

9.45   Dennis and Eugene depart for Portmarnock Golf Club.

10.35   Paddy Galvin, Brian Brown and Jimmy Kinsella meet Dennis and Eugene. Eugene is asked by Dennis to caddy for him. He is honoured (like hell).

1.20   The golf has finished and Dennis, Eugene, Paddy, Brian and Jimmy have sandwiches in the club house.

3.20   Dennis and Eugene depart from Dublin airport for Cork.

4.00   Dennis and Eugene are met at Cork airport by Liam O'Connor and Noel Maginer. All four leave by limo.

4.20   Dennis and Eugene check into the hotel. Dennis has a quick change.

4.40   All four leave for the City Hall, where Dennis is introduced to the Lord Mayor and is presented with some mementoes of Cork.

5.25   Dennis is taken for an interview to the local radio station.

5.50   Dennis returns to hotel for a short nap. Eugene goes to the Neptune Stadium where people have started to queue.

7.45   Dennis, Eugene and Paddy Comerford, the

	referee, are collected by limo for the exhibition.
8.00	The Cork Butter brass band are playing. The atmosphere is electric. Dennis is introduced and gets a standing ovation from some 3,500 fans (probably the biggest ever recorded crowd at any snooker match, beating one between Davis and Higgins in Scotland in 1981). He is presented with some wonderful gifts.
1.40	Dennis departs for the hotel, where he is sat down for a well-deserved meal.
3.00	Dennis retires to bed.
4.00	Eugene retires to bed.

THURSDAY 20 JUNE

7.00	Eugene is awoken by phone calls from Press etc.
9.45	Dennis intends to have a few holes of golf, but it is raining, so he goes to kiss the Blarney Stone.
2.15	Dennis and Eugene check out of the hotel and leave for Cork airport.
3.10	Flight departs for Dublin.
4.00	Flight arrives and Jimmy Kinsella awaits Dennis and Eugene in the V.I.P. lounge. Drinks are served and Dennis rings his manager in London.
4.25	Dennis and Eugene leave Dublin airport.
4.45	Dennis and Eugene arrive at Mosney Holiday centre. There are 600 fans, things are disorganised. Dennis plays one frame, no lighting over the table, a noisy audience, etc. Dennis is not too happy, and is not looking forward to coming back on Sunday.
5.30	Depart from Mosney.

6.00	Dennis and Eugene arrive at Carrickdale hotel on the Newry-Dundalk border and are met by John O'Reilly and Pat Larkin. Dennis is served with a lovely meal in his room before having a short nap. Eugene joins John and Pat for a meal and to discuss final arrangements for the exhibition.
7.45	Dennis and Eugene travel to Newry in John's car.
8.05	The exhibition commences and all runs smoothly. The exhibition finishes about 11 o'clock and Dennis signs autographs for a thousand people.
12.00	Dennis and company arrive back at the hotel, where he has a meal with about fifteen guests.
2.00	Dennis and Eugene retire to bed.

FRIDAY 21 JUNE

9.00	Breakfast is served in the dining-room.
10.00	Dennis and Eugene leave for Coalisland.
10.45	Arrival in Coalisland, Dennis is greeted by his family. It is his first visit back to the house as World Champion.
11.00	Donald Trelford, Editor of the *Observer* in London, arrives at the Taylor home and interviews Dennis and his family for a book he is writing.
2.00	Lunch is served by Jean, Dennis's sister, who now looks after their Dad. Dennis remains in the family home for the afternoon and is informed of the death of a young man whom he saw on his last visit just three weeks ago.
6.45	Eugene collects Dennis and takes him to Gervin's snooker club and talks briefly about

arrangements for the next day. Dennis informs Eugene that he will sit in the back of the car with Donald on the way to Dublin so that he can be interviewed, and asks Eugene to give them a smooth ride, as he is a very jumpy driver.

7.00   300 children are in the club and Dennis plays two frames and some trick shots. History is nearly made as Dennis pots 14 reds and 14 blacks and looks set for a maximum, despite the noisy children who clap as each ball is potted.

8.30   Dennis begins another exhibition for about 250 adults and receives more presentations.

1.00   Eugene takes Dennis to the family home.

SATURDAY 22 JUNE

8.40   Eugene collects Dennis and Donald and sets off on the three-hour journey for Dublin.

11.40   Arrival at the first club in Dublin. Donald leaves for lunch with the Taoisach, nearly without his briefcase. Dennis has a quick cup of tea before playing two frames in front of 300 people.

12.45   Dennis, Eugene, Jimmy and Raymond O'Hara go to the *Irish Independent* office for lunch and meet about 150 people.

2.00   Dennis, Eugene, Jimmy and a secretary, Neave, go to Brown Thomas shop, where Dennis is presented with a beautiful piece of Galway crystal. He meets about 200 people and signs autographs.

3.00   The same party arrive at the E.S.B. club where Dennis is shown how the electricity load pattern was boosted on the night of the final. He is presented with another lovely piece of crystal and plays two frames for an audience of about 500 fans.

4.15 Dennis, Jimmy, Eugene and Neave go back to the hotel, where they relax with a bottle of champagne.

7.45 The show is on the road again, so they collect Paddy Comerford, the referee and off to Ballymun.

8.15 Ballymun snooker centre is the next venue, 600-700 fans are queuing outside. Dennis and company are escorted into the club by Garda. The manager of the club wants to take some photographs with the immediate family (150 of them – quite a large family) before he lets the fans in. Dennis plays two frames and gets another presentation.

9.00 The visit is over. Dennis is escorted back to the car by the Garda. The referee is slow about getting to the car, but arrives minus his mac.

9.25 Arrival at the Swords snooker club ahead of schedule, where there are tea and sandwiches laid on. Dennis is presented with a clock and then plays two frames for an audience of 300.

11.30 Arrival back at the Burlington hotel. Dennis, Eugene, Jimmy, Paddy, Cluther Mooney and his girlfriend relax for a meal and a couple of drinks.

3.00 Dennis retires to bed.

SUNDAY 23 JUNE

1.15 Dennis, Eugene, Jimmy and Paddy leave for Mosney.

2.15	Arrival at Mosney. This time it is well organised. Dennis plays two frames plus trick shots for 600 fans and signs autographs.
4.20	Depart from Mosney.
5.00	Arrival back at hotel.
6.45	Depart for Lucan.
7.15	Dennis and company arrive at Raphells snooker club in Lucan, plays two frames and signs autographs. 200 fans inside and about same outside.
8.10	Depart from Lucan.
8.45	Dennis, Eugene and Jimmy go to the Berkeley Court hotel. The manager treats Dennis and Co. to a drink and shows Dennis the very plush suite.
9.30	Depart from Berkeley Court.
10.00	Dennis and Co. arrive at Joe Nagle's house in Bray, where Joe and his family have invited about fifteen friends. A meal is served and Dennis mingles in the company before finishing the night with some trick shots. A very enjoyable evening.
1.45	Dennis and Eugene say goodbye to Joe and friends and leave for the hotel.

MONDAY 24 JUNE

8.15	Dennis leaves the hotel with Peter Nicolls to play golf for charity. Eugene stays at the hotel to make some phone calls and get Dennis's suits cleaned, etc.
5.30	Dennis arrives back at the hotel and organises an invitation to the charity golfing dinner for Eugene and Jimmy. Dennis takes a nap.
8.30	Dennis, Eugene and Jimmy join directors and

guests of Benson and Hedges for dinner. Dennis starts an auction with a cue which fetches £500 and he is presented with a piece of Waterford crystal.

2.15   Dennis retires to bed.

TUESDAY 25 JUNE

7.00   Eugene takes the luggage to the car.
8.10   Dennis and Eugene leave for Dublin airport.
8.50   Arrival at Dublin airport.
9.00   Eugene says goodbye to Dennis and heads north to Draperstown. Dennis flies to London for yet another appointment.

A tough week for a world champion.

The Far East tour has taken us to Singapore, Malaysia, Hong Kong, Thailand and Communist China. There are promising young players in all these places. Entrants for the world amateur championship now come from over twenty countries. They are white, yellow, brown, even black – and the Chinese are red. All we need are some blues and some greens from outer space. Barry Hearn has been trying to spread the game to Brazil and South America.

It's a much wider world than when I was a boy, cadging games at Jim-Joe Gervin's. The whole continent of Europe beckons. The United States remains the hardest nut to crack because of pool, but the Canadian Open, scene of one of my early triumphs, is being revived, and Australia is picking up again.

After the world final I had heard from people as far away as Greece and Gibraltar. Some had sat round hotel swimming-pools with transistors. Even when Trish and I escaped to Cyprus for a break, we were recognised and I found myself conducting the band of the Irish Guards. At a hotel in Killarney we met my old idols, Joe Dolan and the Drifters, and joined in an Irish sing-song till dawn. When we saw it was 7.30 a.m. and breakfast wasn't being served until 8 o'clock, Joe and I played a frame of snooker to pass the time. We had another hilarious night with the Dublin City Ramblers.

Everywhere I go now I meet strangers who want to shake my hand. I can't buy a cup of coffee without the waitress wanting my autograph. It's all very bewildering for a shy lad from Coalisland, but I can't pretend I don't like it. My win that night seemed to give so many people so much pleasure that they regard me almost as their personal friend.

I remember that when I first arrived in England I was struck by the fact that people didn't say hello to each other in the street. I didn't like it. It seemed so impersonal and unfriendly. For the first seventeen years of my life I'd hardly ever seen a stranger. We all knew each other in Coalisland, so naturally we greeted each other every day. It has taken a long time, but at last the English feel they know me well enough to say hello – even if I don't know them from Adam!

People say there's so much money around in snooker now that the game will be spoilt. That needn't happen at all, unless people are greedy and short-sighted, and the professional body is too experienced to allow that to happen. A game that has struggled against failure only recently can surely cope with success.

What people like about snooker are the best things in it, not the worst. They like the skill, the subtlety, the formality, the colour, the clash of personality, the gladiatorial contest. The drugs, the sex, the drink, the fights, the jealousies and the tantrums are bound to catch the headlines from time to time, because snooker players are human like everybody else. They often come from less privileged backgrounds and many have had the proverbial misspent youth. They also work late at night in an alcoholic atmosphere, often under great personal strain, away from their wives and families. And there'll always be a market for dirt.

If I've brought anything to this game, I hope it's a sense of humour and a touch of common humanity. I'm not larger than life like Hurricane Higgins or Steve Davis in their different ways: I'm life-size like the rest of the world. If I had to guess why my victory had such remarkable popular appeal, I'd say it was because I'd shown that an ordinary man from an ordinary family can do extraordinary things – if he can make the most of his abilities, come to terms with his own strengths and weaknesses, and has the love and support to sustain him through long years of hope and disappointments.

One reason for writing this book is the chance it gives me to say thank-you to the many people who have helped to sustain me in this way – most of all to Trish and the children, to my parents, to my brothers and sisters, my aunts, and to dozens of friends in the snooker world, famous and unknown, who have always kept faith with me over the years.

I've done all my worrying about snooker now. I'm just going to enjoy it and take things as they come. I love being introduced as champion of the world and I'll fight to retain that honour. But I'm not going to let the pressure of that worry me either. I'll give a hundred per cent, as I've always done, and if that's not enough then I'll just have to grin and bear it. If I'm to be remembered for anything at all, I'd like it to be as the man who put the smile back into snooker.